George Albert Smith

The Rise, Progress, and Travels of the Church of Jesus Christ

George Albert Smith

The Rise, Progress, and Travels of the Church of Jesus Christ

ISBN/EAN: 9783742813947

Manufactured in Europe, USA, Canada, Australia, Japa

Cover: Foto ©Lupo / pixelio.de

Manufactured and distributed by brebook publishing software
(www.brebook.com)

George Albert Smith

The Rise, Progress, and Travels of the Church of Jesus Christ

THE

RISE, PROGRESS AND TRAVELS

OF THE

CHURCH OF JESUS CHRIST OF LATTER-DAY SAINTS,

BEING

A SERIES OF

ANSWERS TO QUESTIONS,

INCLUDING

THE REVELATION ON CELESTIAL MARRIAGE,

AND

A Brief Account of the Settlement of Salt Lake Valley, with Interesting Statistics,

BY PRESIDENT GEORGE A. SMITH,

CHURCH HISTORIAN, ETC.

———— ◦❈◦ ————

PRINTED AT THE
DESERET NEWS OFFICE, SALT LAKE CITY:
1869.

PREFACE.

As President Brigham Young and the Church authorities are frequently called upon for information pertaining to the Church history, also the history and settlement of these valleys of the mountains, with the educational, agricultural, horticultural, and irrigation statistics pertaining thereto, &c., it has been deemed wisdom to write and collate such items as would satisfactorily answer the generality of questions propounded; hence, the publication of this pamphlet has been undertaken, with the sincere hope that all honest inquirers after the truth of the Latter-day Work and the material development of the resources of these mountains may be refreshed and gratified by the perusal thereof.

HISTORIAN'S OFFICE,
  Salt Lake City, July, 1869.

ANSWERS TO QUESTIONS

CONCERNING THE

RISE, PROGRESS AND TRAVELS

OF THE

CHURCH OF JESUS CHRIST OF LATTER-DAY SAINTS.

———◇◇◇———

IN THE Spring of 1844, Joseph Smith, President of the Church of Jesus Christ of Latter-day Saints, who was then living at Nauvoo, Hancock county, Illinois, selected a company of men to explore the Rocky Mountains, with a view to find a place where the Saints could locate and enjoy an immunity from that religious persecution which had followed the Church in the States of New York, Ohio, Missouri and Illinois. President Smith at that time expressed his determination to explore the mountain valleys, and prophesied that within five years the Saints would be located in the Rocky Mountains beyond the influence of mobs, requesting it to be recorded, that when it came to pass it might be remembered.

While this company were making preparations for their journey a mob assembled at Carthage, the county seat of Hancock, to menace the Saints. Disappointed political demagogues, writhing under the sting of defeat, and apostates, who had been expelled the Church because of their iniquity, combined at this juncture to fan the flame of excitement and persecution, insomuch that the Governor of the State, Thomas Ford, deemed it advisable to visit Hancock county. When Joseph Smith, the Prophet, learned that the Governor had called out the militia at Carthage, who composed the mob previously collected there, and had made a requisition for additional forces from Warsaw, where resided many of the most bitter enemies of the Saints, he was apprehensive that it was their intention to murder instead of try him, (having already been about fifty times before judicial tribunals, and invariably acquitted) he hesitated to answer the process of law; until the Governor plighted the faith of the State that he should be protected and have a fair trial. When Governor Ford made the pledge, Joseph, with his brother Hyrum, proceeded to Carthage, where they surrendered themselves prisoners to the constable who held the writ for them. They voluntarily entered into recognizances before the Justice of the Peace for their appearance at court to answer the charge; whereupon, a new writ was issued against them on the affidavit of two dissolute men, charging them with *treason*, and they were immediately thrust into jail, Elders Willard Richards and John Taylor being permitted to accompany them.

Governor Ford then disbanded all his troops except the "Carthage Greys," who were known to possess the most violent feelings of hatred against Joseph and Hyrum Smith, and after holding a private council on the subject, he left them to their fate.

MASSACRE OF JOSEPH AND HYRUM SMITH.

On the 27th of June, 1844, about 150 men, with their faces blackened, surrounded the prison and deliberately murdered Joseph and Hyrum Smith, leaving Elder John Taylor severely wounded with four balls, Elder Willard Richards, who was in the same room, escaped unhurt.

At the fall term of court, bills of indictment for murder in the first degree, were found against the principal leaders in the massacre; but they were allowed to go at large on bail and to become each other's security, the sum required being only one thousand dollars.

In May, 1845, they had a sham trial and were acquitted, although the most of the members of the court, bar, jury and witnesses knew them to be guilty of the murder.

The Twelve Apostles, being the first quorum remaining in the Church, immediately returned from their missions abroad, and by the unanimous voice of the Saints took their position at the head of affairs in Nauvoo, Brigham Young, President of the Twelve Apostles, presiding. A revelation had been given through Joseph Smith in 1841, commanding the Saints to build a Temple in which to administer the ordinances of the gospel; also to build a house to be called "The Nauvoo House," for the entertainment of strangers, and a sufficient time was granted for the completion of this work which would be acceptable only in the day of their poverty, in order that they might prove themselves faithful in all things that they were commanded; nevertheless the Lord said:

"Verily, verily I say unto you, that when I give a commandment to any of the sons of men to do a work unto my name, and those sons of men go with all their might and with all they have to perform that work, and cease not their diligence, and their enemies come upon them and hinder them from performing that work, behold it behooveth me to require that work no more at the hands of those sons of men, but to accept of their offerings, and the iniquity and transgression of my holy laws and commandments I will visit upon the heads of those who hindered my work, unto the third and fourth generation, so long as they repent not, and hate me, saith the Lord God. Therefore, for this cause have I accepted the offerings of those whom I commanded to build up a city and a house unto my name, in Jackson County, Missouri, and were hindered by their enemies, saith the Lord your God; and I will answer judgment, wrath and indignation, wailing and anguish, and gnashing of teeth upon their heads unto the third and fourth generation, so long as they repent not and hate me, saith the Lord your God.

"And this I make an example unto you, for your consolation, concerning all those who have been commanded to do a work and have been hindered by the hands of their enemies and by oppression, saith the Lord your God; for I am the Lord your God, and will save all those of your brethren who have been pure in heart and have been slain in the land of Missouri, saith the Lord."

In view of fulfilling this Revelation, the Twelve pushed forward the building of the Temple, which at the time of the Prophet's death was about one half story above the basement. This magnificent work was vigorously prosecuted to its completion in the face of relentless persecution, and amid obstacles of the most difficult and trying kind. A Seventies' Hall, a Music Hall and an Arsenal were also built, the Nauvoo House was recommenced and the brick work of the first story completed; when the mob, coming to the conclusion that the murder of the Prophets had not destroyed the progress of the work of the Lord, commenced, on the 13th of September, 1845, burning houses in the south-west portion of Hancock county, whereupon the sheriff issued the following

PROCLAMATION

To THE CITIZENS OF HANCOCK COUNTY:

Whereas, a mob of from one to two hundred men, under arms, have gathered themselves together in the south-west part of Hancock county, and are at this time destroying the dwellings and other buildings, stacks of grain and other property, of a portion of our citizens, in the most inhuman manner, compelling defenceless children and women to leave their sick beds, and exposing them to the rays of the parching sun, there to lie and suffer without the aid or assistance of a friendly hand to minister to their wants, in their suffering condition.

The rioters spare not the widow nor orphan, and while I am writing this proclamation, the smoke is rising to the clouds and the flames are devouring four buildings which have just been set on fire by the rioters. Thousands of dollars' worth of property has already been consumed, an entire settlement of about sixty or seventy families laid waste, the inhabitants thereof are fired upon, narrowly escaping with their lives, and forced to flee before the ravages of the mob.

By the revised laws of our State under the Criminal Code, sixth division, 58 section, page 181, the crime of Arson is defined as follows: "Every person who "shall wilfully and maliciously burn, or cause to be burned, any dwelling "house, kitchen, office, shop, barn, stable, store-house, etc., etc., shall be deemed "guilty of arson, and upon conviction thereof, shall be punished by imprison- "ment in the penitentiary for a term not less than one year, nor more than "ten years, and should the life or lives of any person or persons be lost in "consequence of any such offense aforesaid, such offender shall be guilty of "murder, and shall be indicted and punished accordingly."

And whereas, the laws of this State make it my duty, as a peace officer of this county, to suppress all riots, routs, etc., etc., and all other crimes,

Therefore, I, J. B. Backenstos, Sheriff of the County of Hancock, and State of Illinois, in the name of the People of said State, and by the authority vested in me by virtue of my office, hereby solemnly command the said rioters and other peace breakers to desist forthwith, disperse, and go to their homes, under penalty of the laws; And I hereby call upon the law-abiding citizens, as a *posse comitatus* of Hancock county, to give their united aid in suppressing the rioters and maintain the supremacy of the law.

> J. B. BACKENSTOS, Sheriff of Hancock County, Illinois.

P. S.—It is a part of my policy, that the citizens of Nauvoo remain quiet and not a man from that city leave as a posse until it be made manifest that the law and order citizens without the city will not have force sufficient to suppress the rioters of this disgraceful outrage, but that 2,000 effective men hold themselves in readiness to march at a moment's warning to any point in Hancock County.

> J. B. B., Sheriff.

Green Plains, Hancock County, Ills., Sept. 13th, 1845.

To this proclamation no attention whatever was paid except by the mob, who used it as a justification for trying to kill the Sheriff, although he was not a "Mormon" and was only acting in the discharge of his official duty. In the attempt, however, to kill the Sheriff, one of the mob was killed.

Subsequently another proclamation was issued calling upon the "Mormon" people of the county as well as all other law-abiding citizens to arm themselves, and be in readiness to act at a moment's notice in the defence of the lives and property of peaceful citizens and to suppress mob violence throughout the county. The leaders of the mob then fled the county to avoid being arrested, upon which Governor Thomas Ford sent Gen. John J. Harding, with 400 militia, to Nauvoo, who dismissed the Sheriff's posse, but made no attempt to arrest the house burners. Gen. Harding informed the Latter-day Saints in Hancock county thåt "the State could not protect them, the mob were determined to drive them from the State, and they must therefore go." Previous to this, a council of the authorities of the Church had passed a resolution which, as a matter of policy, was kept private, to send one thousand five hundred men as pioneers to make a settlement in the valley of the Great Salt Lake, being determined, in accordance with the design and policy of Joseph Smith the Prophet, to leave Illinois.

Meantime a proposition was made to the mob (the State authorities saying they were powerless) to cease vexatious law-suits, stop burning and plundering, and aid the "Mormon" people by purchasing their property on fair terms, allowing them a reasonable time, and they would remove from the State. This proposition was accepted, and in accordance therewith companies were immediately formed, the construction of several thousand wagons was commenced, and during the winter of 1845-46 and the ensuing spring they were built, principally of green timber, which was boiled in brine to facilitate its seasoning. All the iron that could be procured was used in their construction, and the deficiency was made up with raw-hides, hickory withes, &c. Nearly all the old wagons in the surrounding country were purchased, and all possible preparations were made by many for an early start in the spring; but the persecution being renewed, in violation of the before named pledge, one thousand families commenced their journey in the month of February, 1846, some crossing the Mississippi on the ice, thinking by so doing to allay the excitement against those who remained.

President Young, and the leaders of the Church, with a scanty outfit, pursued their journey westward, having to make the road for about three hundred miles through an unsettled country, bridging numerous streams and encountering nearly every vicissitude of weather, making a settlement called Garden Grove on the east fork, and one called Pisgah on the west fork, of Grand river, in the State of Iowa, breaking and planting a thousand acres of prairie land for the benefit of those who were not able to go farther, as well as those who were coming after.

MORMON BATTALION.

The advanced companies arrived at Council Bluffs in July, where they were met by Capt. James Allen of the U. S. army, who called upon them, in behalf of the War Department, for five hundred men to assist in the war with Mexico. Prest. Young's reply to this requisition was, "You shall have your battalion, if it has to be composed of our Elders."

The required battalion was soon made up and on the way, leaving their families in the Omaha country on the west side of the Missouri river in wagons, without protectors or adequate means of subsistence. Thus was this body of volunteers enlisted from the camp of the Latter-day Saints just after their expulsion from Illinois.

There were about two thousand wagons encamped in Western Iowa, between the east fork of Grand river and the Missouri river, a distance of about one hundred and thirty miles; but the main body of the camp was in the Omaha country, on the west side of the Missouri.

The five companies of volunteers assembled at Council Bluffs and were mustered into service on the 16th of July, 1846; they numbered upwards of five hundred men. They marched to Fort Leavenworth, where they received their muskets and other accoutrements of United States infantry.

On the 13th of August they started for California, *via* Santa Fe, each soldier carrying his musket, his blanket, knapsack, ammunition and canteen.

Lieut. Col. Allen, who remained behind the battalion at Fort Leavenworth to complete his outfit, died suddenly; his loss was deeply mourned by the battalion, who were sincerely attached to him. On their march they suffered much for want of water and provisions; in one instance, they traveled sixty miles without water. They arrived at Santa Fe, Sept. 12th, where Lieut. Col. P. St. George Cooke, who had been appointed by Gen. Kearney, took command of the battalion in the place of Col. Allen, deceased, and who, before marching for California, selected out all the laundresses, and those who, on a rigid examination, were supposed to be unable to continue the march, and placed them under the command of Capt. James Brown, who started on the 18th, with orders to make a post at Pueblo on the Arkansas river, which was accordingly done. Col. Cooke, with the battalion, proceeded to California. To avoid the snows of the Rocky Mountains, the battalion followed the Rio Del Norte south for three hundred miles, then turning west, passed through the fortified town of Tucson; after which their guides were unacquainted with the route, and it had to be sought out like men traveling in the dark.

On leaving Santa Fe they were placed on three-quarter rations, and were soon after reduced to one-half and subsequently to one-quarter rations; their meat was composed of the remains of such draft animals as were unable to proceed further. On one occasion, however, they were relieved by a very romantic and providential encounter with a herd of wild bulls. They traveled one hundred miles without water; sank deep wells in the desert, and arrived on the Pacific coast with but little loss. The Colonel issued the following complimentary order on their arrival:

"HEADQUARTERS, Mission of San Diego, Jan. 30th, 1847.

ORDER No. 1.

The Lieut. Colonel commanding congratulates the Battalion on its safe arrival on the shores of the Pacific Ocean, and the conclusion of its march of over two thousand miles. History may be searched in vain for an equal march of infantry; nine-tenths of it through a wilderness, where nothing but savages and wild beasts are found; or deserts where, for the want of water, there is no living creature. There, with almost hopeless labor, we have dug deep wells, which the future traveler will enjoy. Without a guide who had traversed them, we have ventured into trackless prairies, where water was not found for

several marches. With crowbar and pick-axe in hand, we have worked our
way over mountains, which seemed to defy aught save the wild goat, and
hewed a passage through a chasm of living rock, more narrow than our
wagons. To bring these first wagons to the Pacific, we have preserved the
strength of the mules by herding them over large tracts, which you have
laboriously guarded without loss.

The garrison of four Presidios of Sonora, concentrated within the walls of
Tucson, gave us no pause; we drove them out with their artillery; but our
intercourse with the citizens was unmarked by a single act of injustice. Thus
marching, half naked and half fed, and living upon wild animals, we have
discovered and made a road of great value to our country.

Arrived at the first settlement of California, after a single day's rest, you
cheerfully turned off from the route to this point of promised repose, to enter
upon a campaign, and meet, as we believed, the approach of the enemy; and
this, too, without even salt to season your sole subsistence of fresh meat.

Lieutenants A. J. Smith and George Stoneman, of the 1st Dragoons, have
shared and given valuable aid in all these labors.

Thus, volunteers, you have exhibited some high and essential qualities of
veterans. But much remains undone. Soon you will turn your strict attention to the drill, to system and order, to forms also, which are all necessary to
the soldier.

By order of Lieut. Col. P. St. George Cooke,
      (Signed) P. C. Merrill, Adjt."

The distance from Council Bluffs, the place of enlistment, to Fort Leavenworth is about 180 miles; from Fort Leavenworth, by the Cimmeron
route, to Santa Fe, 700 miles; from Santa Fe, by the route traveled to San
Diego, 1150 miles, making a total of 2030 miles. Almost the entire march
being over an uninhabited region, and much of the way a trackless, un-
explored and forbidding desert, affording neither water nor grass sufficient for animals, and, when the teams failed, the battalion had to carry
the extra amount of ammunition and, at the same time, push the wagons
through the heavy sand and over the rugged mountains.

A fruitful source of annoyance to the battalion was the lack of confidence
in the United States Surgeon, Dr. Sanderson, who was known formerly to
have been a bitter persecutor of the Latter-day Saints, and whose expres-
sions and actions confirmed the suspicions that it was his wish to destroy
them; the refusal of many of them to take his prescriptions produced very
unpleasant and angry feelings.

The battalion was discharged at Los Angeles, one year from the date
of their enlistment, without means to enable them to return to their families. At the request of the military commander in California, who feared
a Spanish revolt, one company re-enlisted for six months, which service
was performed in a highly satisfactory manner, both to the officers and the
people of San Diego where they were stationed.

WINTER QUARTERS.

After the departure of the battalion from Council Bluffs, Prest. Young
gathered up the scattering companies and established a town called Winter Quarters, where 700 log cabins and 150 dug-outs (cabins half under
ground) were built during the Fall and Winter, upon the site of what is
now known as Florence, Nebraska. At this point the Saints suffered ex-
tremely from sickness, exposure and the want of the necessaries of life.
Several thousand wagons were also encamped in various localities on the

east side of the Missouri river, where the Saints began to build up a place, subsequently named Kanesville, in honor of Thomas L. Kane, of Philadelphia, whose kindness had endeared him to them.

EXPULSION FROM NAUVOO.

When it became known in Illinois that the flower of the camp had enlisted into the service of the United States, the mob assembled with redoubled fury, formed a military encampment, provided with artillery, in the neighborhood of Nauvoo, which now contained the poor, the helpless, the sick and infirm, as all who were able to leave, on any terms, had done so during the Spring and Summer.

The mob, under command of Rev. Thomas S. Brockman, increased their force to about 1800, made several unsuccessful attacks upon the city, (which could barely muster 123 men) killing three men and wounding a number of others and battering down many buildings. They finally succeeded, on the 17th day of September, after several days' siege and three days' bombardment, in driving the people, helpless and destitute of everything that could make life desirable, across the river into Iowa. Here many must have perished from starvation had not the kind Creator fed them by sending upon their camps flocks of quails so tame that the women caught them with their hands. In this place they lay exposed to the storms of autumn right in view of a thousand empty houses belonging to themselves and friends, until teams were sent back from the camps to remove the survivors, many having died. To crown their victory, the mob subsequently set fire to the Temple of Nauvoo, which was the most beautiful building in the Western States. It was the first specimen of a new order of architecture, introduced by President Joseph Smith, and had cost a million dollars. The light of its fire was visible for thirty miles.

Very little real estate had been sold, though the improvements, property and buildings of the Saints in Illinois were among the best in the Western States. Such a vast amount of property exposed for sale in Hancock and the adjoining counties had a tendency to glut the market, which, together with the hostile influence of our enemies, prevented sales even at low rates. Fortunately oxen were cheap, and companies continued leaving till late in the summer, making the new route a grand encampment for 300 miles, as wagons were to be seen at every watering place.

For a more full description of these scenes, the following extract is copied from the historical address of Colonel (now General) Thomas L. Kane, who was an eye-witness:

"A few years ago," said Colonel Kane, "ascending the Upper Mississippi in the autumn, when its waters were low, I was compelled to travel by land past the region of the Rapids. My road lay through the Half-Breed Tract, a fine section of Iowa, which the unsettled state of its land-titles had appropriated as a sanctuary for coiners, horse thieves, and other outlaws. I had left my steamer at Keokuk, at the foot of the Lower Fall, to hire a carriage, and to contend for some fragments of a dirty meal with the swarming flies, the only scavengers of the locality.

"From this place to where the deep water of the river returns, my eye wearied to see everywhere sordid, vagabond and idle settlers; and a country marred, without being improved, by their careless hands. I was descending the last hill-side upon my journey, when a landscape in delightful contrast broke upon my view. Half encircled by a bend of the river, a beautiful city lay glittering in the fresh morning sun; its bright new dwellings, set in cool green gardens, ranging up around a stately dome-shaped hill, which was crowned by a noble edifice, whose high tapering spire was radiant with white and gold. The city appeared to cover several miles; and beyond it, in the back-ground, there rolled off a fair country, chequered by the careful lines of fruitful husbandry. The unmistakeable marks of industry, enterprise, and educated wealth everywhere, made the scene one of singular and most striking beauty. It was a natural impulse to visit this inviting region. I procured a skiff, and rowing across the river, landed at the chief wharf of the city. No one met me there. I looked, and saw no one. I could hear no one move; though the quiet everywhere was such that I heard the flies buzz, and the water-ripples break against the shallow of the beach. I walked through the solitary streets. The town lay as in a dream, under some deadening spell of loneliness, from which I almost feared to wake it; for plainly it had not slept long. There was no grass growing up in the paved ways; rains had not entirely washed away the prints of dusty footsteps.

"Yet I went about unchecked. I went into empty workshops, rope-walks and smithies. The spinner's wheel was idle; the carpenter had gone from his work-bench and shavings, his unfinished sash and casing. Fresh bark was in the tanner's vat, and the fresh-chopped lightwood stood piled against the baker's oven. The blacksmith's shop was cold; but his coal heap, and ladling pool, and crooked water horn, were all there, as if he had just gone off for a holiday. No work-people anywhere looked to know my errand.

"If I went into the gardens, clinking the wicket-latch loudly after me, to pull the marygolds, heartsease, and lady-slippers, and draw a drink with the water-sodden well-bucket and its noisy chain; or, knocking off with my stick the tall, heavy-headed dahlias and sunflowers, hunted over the beds for cucumbers and love-apples—no one called out to me from any opened window, or dog sprang forward to bark an alarm.

"I could have supposed the people hidden in the houses, but the doors were unfastened; and when at last I timidly entered them, I found dead ashes white upon the hearths, and had to tread a-tiptoe, as if walking down the aisle of a country church, to avoid arousing irreverent echoes from the naked floors. On the outskirts of the town was the city graveyard; but there was no record of plague there, nor did it in anywise differ much from other Protestant American cemeteries. Some of the mounds were not long sodded; some of the stones were newly set, their dates recent, and their black inscriptions glossy in the mason's hardly dried lettering ink. Beyond the graveyard, out in the fields, I saw, in one spot hard by where the fruited boughs of a young orchard had been roughly torn down, the still smouldering embers of a barbecue fire, that had been constructed of rails from the fencing around it. It was the latest sign of life there. Fields upon fields of heavy-headed yellow grain lay rotting ungathered upon the ground. No one was at hand to take in their rich harvest.

"As far as the eye could reach, they stretched away—they, sleeping too in the hazy air of autumn. Only two portions of the city seemed to suggest the import of this mysterious solitude. On the southern suburb, the houses looking out upon the country showed, by their splintered woodwork and walls battered to the foundation, that they had lately been the mark of a destructive cannonade. And in and around the splendid Temple, which had been the chief object of my admiration, armed men were barracked, surrounded by their stacks of musketry and pieces of heavy ordnance. These challenged me to render an account of myself and why I had had the temerity to cross the water without a written permit from a leader of their band.

"Though these men were generally more or less under the influence of ardent spirits, after I had explained myself as a passing stranger, they seemed anxious to gain my good opinion. They told the story of the Dead City; that it had been a notable manufacturing and commercial mart, sheltering over 20,000 persons; that they had waged war with its inhabitants for several years, and had been finally successful only a few days before my visit, in an action fought in front of the ruined suburb; after which, they had driven them forth at the point of the sword. The defence, they said, had been obstinate, but gave way on the third day's bombardment. They boasted greatly of their prowess, especially in this battle, as they called it; but I discovered they were not of one mind as to certain of the exploits that had distinguished it, one of which, as I remember, was, that they had slain a father and his son, a boy of fifteen, not long residents of the fated city, whom they admitted to have borne a character without reproach.

"They also conducted me inside the massive sculptured walls of the curious Temple, in which they said the banished inhabitants were accustomed to celebrate the mystic rites of an unhallowed worship. They particularly pointed out to me certain features of the building, which, having been the peculiar objects of a former superstitious regard, they had, as a matter of duty, sedulously defiled and defaced. The reputed sites of certain shrines they had thus particularly noticed; and various sheltered chambers, in one of which was a deep well, constructed, they believed, with a dreadful design. Beside these, they led me to see a large and deep-chiselled marble vase or basin, supported upon twelve oxen, also of marble, and of the size of life, of which they told some romantic stories. They said the deluded persons, most of whom were emigrants from a great distance, believed their Deity countenanced their reception here of a baptism of regeneration, as proxies for whomsoever they held in warm affection in the countries from which they had come. That here parents 'went into the water' for their lost children, children for their parents, widows for their spouses, and young persons for their lovers; that thus the Great Vase came to be for them associated with all dear and distant memories, and was therefore the object, of all others in the building, to which they attached the greatest degree of idolatrous affection. On this account, the victors had so diligently desecrated it, as to render the apartment in which it was contained too noisome to abide in.

"They permitted me also to ascend into the steeple, to see where it had been lightning-struck on the Sabbath before; and to look out, east and south, on wasted farms like those I had seen near the city, extending till they were lost in the distance. Here, in the face of pure day, close to the scar of the divine wrath left by the thunderbolt, were fragments of food, cruses of liquor, and broken drinking vessels, with a bass drum and a steamboat signal bell, of which I afterwards learned the use with pain

"It was after nightfall, when I was ready to cross the river on my return. The wind had freshened since the sunset, and the water beating roughly into my little boat, I headed higher up the stream than the point I had left in the morning, and landed where a faint glimmering light invited me to steer.

"Here, among the dock and rushes, sheltered only by the darkness, without roof between them and the sky, I came upon a crowd of several hundred human creatures, whom my movements roused from uneasy slumber upon the ground.

"Passing these on my way to the light, I found it came from a tallow candle, in a paper funnel shade, such as is used by street vendors of apples and peanuts, and which, flaring and guttering away in the bleak air off the water, shone flickeringly on the emaciated features of a man in the last stage of a billous, remittent fever. They had done their best for him. Over his head was something like a tent, made of a sheet or two, and he rested on a but partially ripped open old straw mattress, with a hair sofa cushion under his head for a pillow. His gaping jaw and glazing eye told how short a time he would monopolize these luxuries; though a seemingly bewildered and excited person, who might have been his wife, seemed to find hope in occasionally forcing him to swallow, awkwardly-measured, sips of the tepid river water, from a burned and battered bitter-smelling tin coffee pot. Those who knew better had furnished the apothecary he needed; a toothless old bald-head, whose manner had the repulsive dullness of a man familiar with death scenes. He, so long as I remained, mumbled in his patient's ear a monotonous and melancholy prayer, between the pauses of which I heard the hiccup and sobbing of two little girls, who were sitting upon a piece of drift wood outside.

"Dreadful, indeed, was the suffering of these forsaken beings; bowed and cramped by cold and sunburn; alternating as each weary day and night dragged on, they were, almost all of them, the crippled victims of disease. They were there because they had no homes, nor hospital, nor poor-house, nor friends to offer them any. They could not satisfy the feeble cravings of their sick; they had not bread to quiet the fractious hunger-cries of their children. Mothers and babes, daughters and grand-parents, all of them alike, were bivouacked in tatters, wanting even covering to comfort those whom the sick shiver of fever were searching to the marrow.

"These were Mormons, famishing in L e county, Iowa, in the fourth week of the month of September, in the year of our Lord 1846. The city—it was Nauvoo, Ill. The Mormons were the owners of that city, and the smiling country around. And those who had stopped their ploughs, who had silenced their hammers, their axes, their shuttles, and their workshop wheels; those who had put out their fires, who had eaten their food, spoiled their orchards, and trampled under foot their thousands of acres of unharvested bread; these were the keepers of their dwellings, the carousers in their temple, whose drunken riot insulted the ears of their dying.

"I think it was as I turned from the wretched night watch of which I have spoken, that I first listened to the sounds of revel of a party of the guard within the city. Above the distant hum of the voices of many, occasionally rose distinct the loud oath-tainted exclamation, and the falsely intonated scrap of vulgar song; but lest this requiem should go unheeded, every now and then, when their boisterous orgies strove to attain a sort of ecstatic climax, a cruel spirit of insulting frolic carried some of them up into the high belfry of the Temple steeple, and there, with the wicked childishness of inebriates, they whooped, and shrieked, and beat the drum that I had seen, and rang in chari-varic unison their loud-tongued steam-boat bell.

"They were, all told, not more than six hundred and forty persons who were thus lying on the river flats. But the Mormons in Nauvoo and its dependencies had been numbered the year before at over twenty thousand. Where were they? They had last been seen, carrying in mournful trains their sick and wounded, halt and blind, to disappear behind the western horizon, pursuing the phantom of another home. Hardly anything else was known of them: and people asked with curiosity, 'What had been their fate—what their fortunes?'"

The rear of the camp of the Saints that were driven out of Nauvoo encamped on the banks of the Mississippi, a very uncomfortable and distressing situation, where they were frequently annoyed by the firing of cannon from the opposite side of the river, many of the shot landing in the river, but occasionally some would pass over into the camp. One of them, picked up in the camp, was sent as a present to the Governor of Iowa.

PIONEERING JOURNEY.

In the spring of 1847, President Brigham Young, with 143 pioneers, started in search of a place of settlement. He was led by the inspiration of the Almighty, (for no one of the company knew anything of the country) directly to Great Salt Lake Valley, where he and the company arrived on the 24th day of July, having sought out and made a new road 650 miles, and followed a trappers' trail nearly 400 miles On the 29th of July the Pioneers received additional strength by the arrival of Captain James Brown and a detachment of the battalion and a company of Saints from the Mississippi, who wintered with the detachment on the Arkansas river. Seven of the detachment died on the route.

SALT LAKE CITY.

The population, being now about four hundred, the building of Salt Lake City was commenced by the erection of a Fort, enclosing ten acres.

The arrival of the Pioneers and this detachment of the battalion, all armed and carrying the flag of the United States, the commencement to build a fort and the hoisting of the stars and stripes (although this country at the time belonged to Mexico) had a tendency to impress the wild tribes of the mountains with respect, and made it comparatively easy to promote friendly relations with them.

The Twelve Apostles organized Salt Lake City into a Stake of Zion and appointed John Smith President; Charles C. Rich and John Young his counsellors; Tarlton Lewis, Bishop, and a High Council. This organization went into effect on the arrival of the immigrant companies in the Fall of 1847, when about 700 wagons laden with families arrived on the site of Salt Lake City.

The whole basin was so barren as to produce little besides a species of bunch grass, and the ground was covered with myriads of large black crickets, which were the food of the Indians. In this desert place the site of Salt Lake City was surveyed.

Not a single person in the whole company had a full supply of provisions, but all were on half rations. About one hundred, who had served in the "Mormon" Battalion, found their way here from California in the Winter, without any provisions.

RETURN OF THE PIONEERS.

On the 25th of August, 1847, President Brigham Young and 107 others started on their return to Winter Quarters. At the South Pass the Sioux Indians stole part of their animals, which compelled them to walk most of the way to the Missouri river, depending mostly upon such game as they could obtain by the way, and being without suitable horses for chasing the buffalo the few obtained were generally old bulls, whose flesh was of very poor quality and not sufficient in quantity to supply their wants.

In 1848, President Young arrived again in Salt Lake valley with about eight hundred wagons.

The crickets, during the season of 1848, came down from the mountains in myriads and destroyed a great portion of the scanty crops; and, notwithstanding every effort was made to drive them off by means of bushes, long rods, &c., whole families and neighborhoods turning out *en masse* until almost exhausted, the whole would have been destroyed had not the Almighty in His kindness sent gulls in vast numbers, covering every field, driving the crickets from the crops into the streams and even into door yards, and devouring them until gorged, then vomiting them and devouring more.

Notwithstanding the "Mormon" Battalion had been in the service of the United States, those of their families which were located at Winter Quarters were required, by the Indian Department, in the Spring of 1848, to leave their cabins and recross the river into Iowa. Yet it was well known they were only encamped there awaiting the return of their husbands, fathers and brothers, who had been discharged on the Pacific coast, without means of transportation or rations.

GOLD DISCOVERED IN CALIFORNIA.

In the Spring of 1848, some members of the "Mormon" Battalion discovered gold in California; thus opening to the world an unparalleled source of wealth and adventure.

LOG TABERNACLE CONFERENCE.

At a General Conference held at the log Tabernacle in December, 1847, at Kanesville, (now Council Bluffs,) Iowa, the Saints acknowledged Brigham Young President of the Church of Jesus Christ of Latter day Saints, and Heber C. Kimball and Willard Richards his counselors. This action was confirmed at the General Conference held in Salt Lake Valley after the companies arrived in the Fall of 1848; John Smith was chosen Patriarch over the whole Church, and in February, 1849, Charles C. Rich, Lorenzo Snow, Erastus Snow and Franklin D. Richards were ordained to fill the Quorum of the Twelve Apostles.

CHURCH AUTHORITIES—1849.

The Church authorities then stood as follows: Brigham Young, President; Heber C. Kimball and Willard Richards, counsellors; Orson Hyde, President of the Twelve Apostles; Parley P. Pratt, Orson Pratt, John Taylor, Wilford Woodruff, George A. Smith, Amasa M. Lyman, Ezra T. Benson, Charles C. Rich, Lorenzo Snow, Erastus Snow and Franklin D. Richards, members of the Quorum of the Twelve; John Smith, Patriarch; Daniel Spencer, President of the Stake of Salt Lake, and Newel K. Whitney, Presiding Bishop.

ORGANIZATION AND CAMP RULES.

The companies for the plains were organized at the Elk Horn river, about 18 miles west of Winter Quarters, now Florence, Nebraska, into companies of hundreds, fifties and tens; each fifty was provided with a blacksmith and wagon maker with tools for repairing wagons and shoeing animals. Three hundred pounds of breadstuff were required for each person emigrating, and a good gun with 100 rounds of ammunition for each able-bodied man. Many cows were worked in the yoke. Each family was also required to take a due proportion of seed grain and agricultural implements. Every wagon, load and team was inspected by a committee, and none were allowed to start on to the plains without the required outfit. A strict guard was kept over the cattle by night and day, and also in the camps, which were formed in an oval shape, the inside making a corral for the stock. Pigs and poultry were carried in coops attached to the wagons.

No person was allowed by the rules to wander about, not even to hunt game, except under special directions, and by these precautions no person was lost and but few accidents occurred, and the loss of animals was small, although we traveled ten hundred and thirty-four miles from the Missouri river to Salt Lake City, through an uninhabited and desert region. Saturday afternoon was usually occupied washing, baking, repairing wagons and shoeing animals, and Sunday was a day of rest and worship. Morning and evening prayers and songs of praise were never omitted in the camps, and occasionally a dance was enjoyed, the companies generally being favored with musical talent.

Thus the refining influences of society and civilization were continually felt and kept in view, and the moral status of the camps preserved inviolate through all the fatigues, hardships, exposures and vexatious annoyances of the entire journey.

BREAD REGULATIONS.

For about three years every head of a family issued his breadstuff in rations daily, varying from one-quarter to one pound per soul, according to the amount of provisions he had on hand; most of the time the rations were from one-half to three-fourths of a pound, sometimes accompanied with vegetables and milk; but if without these, the bread was not increased, for it was necessary that it should be made to last until harvest. This order of things continued until the population increased to over 12000, when in 1850 an abundant harvest put an end to the necessity of rationing. In 1855, most of the crops were destroyed by grasshoppers and drouth, compelling the people to subsist principally upon the surplus of previous years, and the adoption again of the system of rationing, which continued until the harvest of 1856. In addition to the loss of crops by grasshoppers, vast numbers of cattle died in consequence of the severity of the winter of 1855-6, materially lessening the quantity of food. During these periods great numbers of gold hunters *en route* for California came into the valley destitute of food, who were fed and aided on their way from our scanty supplies. In all these times of scarcity measures were taken to supply those who were unable to furnish themselves. Fast days were proclaimed in all the congregations on the first Thursday of each month, and the food saved in that way distributed among the poor; and thousands of persons who had an abundance of bread put their families on rations, so as to save the same for those who could not otherwise obtain it. And so wise and liberal were the regulations during these periods of scarcity incident upon settling the Territory that no one perished or even suffered materially for the want of food, and all were remarkably healthy.

CIVIL GOVERNMENT.—STATE OF DESERET.

In March, 1849, a Provisional Government was organized and a State Constitution adopted by a convention under the name of "The State of Deseret." A delegate was sent to Congress, with a petition for admission into the Union. At the first general election, a Governor, Secretary, Chief Justice and two Associates, Marshal, Attorney General, Assessor and Collector, Treasurer and Magistrates were elected.

Under the Provisional Government of the State of Deseret, and before the Territorial Organic Act passed, the counties of Salt Lake, Davis, Weber, Utah, Sanpete and Iron were organized, and the cities of Salt Lake, Ogden, Provo, Manti and Parowan were incorporated. Bridges were constructed across the Weber, Ogden and Provo rivers, and two across the Jordan river; new valleys were explored and roads opened into various parts of the State, all of which were free from toll, although costing an immense amount of labor, in consequence of the rugged features of the country, the great difficulty in getting timber, and the scarcity of saw mills.

Although the country was one of the most barren by nature ever inhabited by man, scarcely a tree or a bush growing below the snow line without irrigation, no colony ever progressed with more equal and uniform rapidity.

TERRITORY OF UTAH.

September 9th, 1850. an act of Congress providing for the organization of the Territorial government of Utah was approved; Sec. 7 of which declares the laws of the United States to be in force in Utah as far as applicable. The judges of the Supreme Court did not enter upon their duties until 1853.

Brigham Young was appointed Governor of Utah by President Millard Fillmore, and continued in office until the arrival of Alfred Cumming, in April, 1858, and performed the duties of that office to the entire satisfaction of the inhabitants, who unanimously desired his re-appointment.

SETTLEMENT OF COUNTIES.

Salt Lake County was settled by President Brigham Young and pioneers who entered Salt Lake Valley, July 24th, 1847. They erected a fort of logs and sun-dried bricks, enclosing ten acres of land, now known as the "old fort" block, in the Sixth Ward of Salt Lake City.

Davis County by Peregrine Sessions, in the Spring of 1848. He located at Bountiful.

Weber County by Capt. James Brown, in the Spring of 1848. He purchased some shanties and a Mexican grant of land from Miles Goodyear, an Indian trader, on the site of Ogden City.

Utah County by John and Isaac Higbee and thirty others, who built a picket fort near the site of Provo City in the Spring of 1849.

Tooele County by John Rowberry and others in 1849.

San Pete County by a company under the guidance of Isaac Morley, Seth Taft and Charles Shumway, who entered that valley in November, 1849, and located at Manti.

December 8, 1850, thirty families left Salt Lake City, including one hundred and eighteen men, with six hundred head of stock and one hundred and one wagons, led by Elder George A. Smith; and in January following arrived at, and settled the county of, Iron, by building a fort at Parowan.

Millard County in the Fall of 1851, by Anson Call and thirty families.

Box Elder County by Simeon A. Carter and others, in 1851.

Carson County (now in the State of Nevada) by Col. John Reese, in 1851, and in 1855 by missionaries from Salt Lake Valley, under the direction of Hon. Orson Hyde, when the county was organized.

Juab County in the Fall of 1852, by Joseph L. Heywood and George W. Bradley, who located at Nephi.

Washington County in the Spring of 1852, by John D. Lee, who made a ranch on Ash Creek. The cotton region of the county by Jacob Hamblin, at Santa Clara, in 1855, Joseph Horn, at Heberville, in 1857, Robert

D. Covington and thirty-three others, at Washington, in 1857, and Joshua T. Willis, at Toquer, in the Spring of 1858.

Summit County in 1853, by Samuel Snyder, Esq., who built saw mills in Parley's Park.

Green River County, now included in Wyoming Territory, by President Brigham Young, who purchased of James Bridger a Mexican grant for thirty miles of land and some cabins, known as Fort Bridger, for which he paid eight thousand dollars in gold; the deeds of this property : re still in his possession. He erected a stone fort and corrals for the protection of animals and made other improvements on the ranch, expending about $8,000 more.

In November, 1853, John Nebeker and a company of thirty-nine brethren, also Isaac Bullock and another company numbering fifty-three men, left Salt Lake and Utah counties and located at Fort Supply, in Green River County. They built houses, fenced and broke up land and planted crops.

In 1857, the United States army, under Gen. Johnson, took possession of Fort Bridger, in the name of the United States, and declared it to be a military reservation. The reservation was also extended over the settlement and farming lands of Fort Supply, the county seat.

Alfred Cumming, then Governor of Utah, made an attempt to restore the property to the citizens who had been dispossessed by military authority but his efforts were unsuccessful, having been overruled by John B. Floyd, then Secretary of War. The loss and damage sustained by these pioneers, were about $300,000.

Morgan County by Jedediah M. Grant and Thomas Thurstin, in the Spring of 1855.

Cache County in 1856, by Peter Maughan and others, at Wellsville.

Beaver County in 1856, by Edward Thompson and thirteen others from Parowan.

Kane County in the Fall of 1858, by Nephi Johnson and six others, who located at Virgen City.

Rich County in 1863, by Elder Charles C. Rich and many others.

Wasatch County by twenty men from Provo and Spanish and American Forks.

TERRITORIAL LEGISLATURE AND CONVENTIONS.

At the first session of the Territorial Legislature, held in 1851-2, in Salt Lake City, memorials to Congress were adopted praying for the construction of a National Central Railroad, and also a telegraph line from the Missouri river, *via* Salt Lake City, to the Pacific.

The Legislature continued to memorialize Congress from time to time on these subjects, until a telegraph line was established, connecting the Atlantic and the Pacific coasts and the great National Central Railroad, so long desired, is now completed.

The following Memorial was signed by Governor Brigham Young:

MEMORIAL TO CONGRESS FOR THE CONSTRUCTION OF A GREAT NATIONAL CENTRAL RAILROAD TO THE PACIFIC COAST.

APPROVED MARCH 3, 1852.

To the Honorable, the Senate and House of Representatives of the United States, in Congress assembled:

Your memorialists, the Governor and Legislative Assembly of the Territory of Utah, respectfully pray your honorable body, to provide for the establishment of a national central railroad from some eligible point on the Mississippi or Missouri rivers, to San Diego, San Francisco, Sacramento or Astoria, or such other point on or near the Pacific coast, as the wisdom of your honorable body may dictate.

Your memorialists respectfully state, that the immense emigration to and from the Pacific, requires the immediate attention, guardian care, and fostering assistance of the greatest and most liberal government on the earth. Your memorialists are of opinion that not less than five thousand American citizens have perished on the different routes within the last three years, for the want of proper means of transportation; that an eligible route can be obtained your memorialists have no doubt, being extensively acquainted with the country. We know, that no obstruction exists between this point and San Diego, and that iron, coal, timber, stone, and other materials exist in various places on the route; and that the settlements of this Territory are so situated, as to amply supply the builders of said road, with materials and provisions for a considerable portion of the route, and to carry on an extensive trade after the road is completed.

Your memorialists are of opinion that the mineral resources of California, and these mountains, can never be fully developed to the benefit of the people of the United States, without the construction of such a road; and, upon its completion, the entire trade of China and the East Indies will pass through the heart of the Union, thereby giving our citizens the almost entire control of the Asiatic and Pacific trade; pouring into the lap of the American States, the millions that are now diverted through other commercial channels: and last, though not least, the road herein proposed would be a perpetual chain, or iron band, which would effectually hold together our glorious Union with an imperishable identity of mutual interest; thereby, consolidating our relations with foreign powers in times of peace and our defence from foreign invasion by the speedy transmission of troops and supplies, in times of war.

The earnest attention of Congress to this important subject is solicited by your memorialists, who, in duty bound, will ever pray.

The Territorial Legislature in December, 1855, passed an act providing for holding a convention to form and adopt a Constitution for the Territory, with a view to its admission into the Union as a State.

The convention met in March and adopted a Constitution, under the name and style of "The State of Deseret," and a memorial to Congress, which were submitted to the people and unanimously approved, and were presented to Congress by the Delegate, Hon. John M. Bernhisel.

In 1862, another convention was held, which re-adopted, with slight amendments, the Constitution of 1856, which was again submitted to the people and approved. A State government was organized, and the General Assembly met and elected Hons. George Q. Cannon and William H. Hooper, Senators to Congress, who went to Washington and endeavored, unsuccessfully, to gain admission as a State.

DELEGATES IN CONGRESS.

The Territorial Delegate from 1851 to 1859 and from 1861 to 1863 was Hon. John M. Bernhisel; from 1863 to 1865, Hon. John F. Kinney; from

1859 to 1861 and from 1865 to 1869, Hon. William H. Hooper, who is the present Delegate.

AREA, AGRICULTURE, ETC., OF UTAH.

Utah extends from the 37th parallel of north latitude to the 42d, and from the 109th to the 114th degree of longitude. The area is about 70,000 square miles. The proportion of land susceptible of cultivation is very small, the general character of the Territory being that of mountain and desert. The Agricultural Society in 1866 reported about 134,000 acres under cultivation. Some tracts of land, apparently fine, rich soil, of superior quality, fail to produce crops, owing to the superabundance of alkali and other mineral substances, which encrust the surface of the earth. The agriculture of the country is carried on at a heavy expense, incurred by irrigation, the land having generally to be watered several times to produce wheat and barley, and oftener for Indian corn and roots.

The necessity of irrigation entails a continual expense upon the agriculturist in cleaning out ditches and canals and repairing dams. On much of the soil the ditches have to be cleaned out twice a year. Good wheat, corn and vegetables may be produced in abundance, if carefully irrigated.

The following tables of the expense of the main irrigating canals and the amount of land irrigated by the same, and agricultural statistics for 1865, serve to show, although very incomplete, the cost, as also the success, attending agricultural industry in Utah.

Number of canals, 277; total length, in rods, 333,862; cost of construction, including dams, $1,766,939; number of acres irrigated, 153,949; estimated cost of canals in progress, $877,730.

	Wheat	Barley	Oats	Corn	Meadow	Sundry small crops	Cotton	Sorghum	Potatoes	Beets	Carrots
Measure or weight.	Bus	Bus	Bus	Bus	Ton	Bus	Lbs	Gal	Bus	Bus	Bus
Average per acre	23	30	31	20	1½	115	151	79	139	265	344
Acres	55,533	4,881	11,631	9,502	65,044	2,421	551	2,888	4,832	305	454

About 115 saw and 90 grist mills are in operation, and three woolen and three cotton mills.

PUBLIC BUILDINGS.

Amongst the public buildings there are the Deseret State House, erected in 1849-50, in Salt Lake City, which has been occupied by the Legislature for about sixteen years, and is now used by the Deseret University. The

Utah Territorial House, at Fillmore City.   The Tabernacle, in Salt Lake City, a building 64x158, arched, without a column.   The New Tabernacle 150x250, 80 feet high, oval in form, without a column, built on stone pillars 22 feet high, the roof being lattice-work of red pine timber, and, with gallery, yet to be constructed, will contain 12,000 people.   The organ in course of erection in this edifice is second to none in the United States, in appearance and sweetness of tone, and is exceeded in size by but one.   It was constructed entirely by Utah mechanics, under the direction of Elder Joseph Ridges.   A small amount of material was imported; the principal part thereof was produced at home.   To hear the melody of the organ richly repays a visit to the Tabernacle.   The Court House is a well finished building, 40x55.   The City Hall, 60x60, built of stone, at a cost of $75,000, with clock and bell.

The Theatre (including addition) is 80 by 172 feet, 46 feet high inside.

There are many imposing edifices in the settlements, principally meeting-houses and county buildings.

COMMON SCHOOLS.

According to the report of Robert L. Campbell, Superintendent of Common Schools, there are 186 school districts in the Territory, with a school population—children between 4 and 16 years—of upwards of 22,000, out of which 58 per cent. are enrolled in school schedules, the actual attendance being about 42 per cent.

The public lands donated by Congress to States and Territories, in the absence of a land office, have not been available, hence there is no public school fund.   Schools, however, are generously supported by the people.

Salt Lake City is divided into twenty one school districts, with a good public school-house in each, some districts having three and four schools; besides which there are private schools and two academies, and two commercial colleges.

NEWSPAPERS AND MAGAZINES.

The following newspapers and magazines are published in Utah :
The "Deseret News," Weekly, Semi-Weekly and Daily, edited by George Q. Cannon; issue, 15,000 copies.   The "Juvenile Instructor," also edited by George Q. Cannon; issue, 3000 copies semi-monthly.   The "Utah Magazine," published by Harrison & Godbe.   The Salt Lake Daily, Semi-Weekly and Weekly "Telegraph," by T. B. H. Stenhouse.   These are published in Salt Lake City.   The "Rio Virgen Times," the "Cactus," and " St. George Juvenile," are published at St. George, in Southern Utah.

DEMISE AND SUCCESSION OF LEADING AUTHORITIES.

Newel K. Whitney, presiding Bishop, died in Salt Lake City, Sept. 23, 1850.   Edward Hunter was appointed his successor.

Elder Willard Richards, one of the First Presidency, Church Historian and Editor of the "Deseret News," died at his residence in Salt Lake City on the 11th of March, 1854, and was succeeded by Elder Jedediah Morgan Grant, as Second Counselor to President Young.

Patriarch John Smith died May 23d, 1854, at his residence in Salt Lake City, and was succeeded by John Smith, (son of Hyrum) who was set apart to the office of Patriarch, Feb. 18th, 1855.

Elder Jedediah Morgan Grant died December 1st, 1856, at his residence in Salt Lake City, and on the 4th day of January, 1857, Elder Daniel H. Wells was chosen to fill the vacancy thus caused in the quorum of the First Presidency.

Elder Heber Chase Kimball, first counselor to President Young, died June 22d, 1868, at his residence in Salt Lake City, and at the Conference of October 6th, 1868, Elder George Albert Smith was appointed to succeed Elder Kimball in the office of First Counselor to President Young.

Daniel Spencer was set apart as President of this Stake of Zion, Feb. 13, 1849. He died in Salt Lake City, Dec. 13, 1868. John W. Young was appointed his successor.

INDIAN OUTRAGES.

The course adopted towards the Indians in Utah has been the peaceful policy of feeding and clothing, in preference to fighting them. A vast amount of labor and means have been expended in locating farms, supplying implements and teaching the art of husbandry to the Indians throughout the Territory, which has been a very heavy tax upon the people.

Almost every difficulty which has existed or arisen between the citizens of the Territory and the Indians has been the result of reckless and barbarous treatment by emigrants passing through the Territory, or by indiscreet and foolish persons residing therein.

A portion of the Utes located in Utah valley became hostile in the Spring of 1849, in consequence of one of their number being killed, which was unknown to the authorities of the Provisional State for some time. This war resulted in the death of Joseph Higbee, the wounding of several others, the expenditure of thousands of dollars in a campaign, suspension of labor, and stock driven off or destroyed. In the Fall of 1850, the Indians in the northern part of the Territory were also hostile from similar causes. A party of emigrants from Missouri, who were encamped on the Malad, shot several squaws who were crossing the stream on horse-back, and took their horses; they then continued their journey westward. When this fact came to the knowledge of the warriors, they made a descent upon the northern settlements, killing Mr. Campbell, who was engaged in erecting a mill. In a short time a company of volunteers were on the spot, and ascertaining the cause of the difficulty, through some friendly Indians, succeeded in restoring peace by paying the Indians for the squaws who had been killed and the horses that had been taken off, and by this means avoided further bloodshed.

In 1853, a person named Ivey, in a passion, struck an Indian, which resulted in his death. A war ensued, which continued about one year, in which a number of persons were killed. Several flourishing settlements on the frontiers had to abandoned and were burned by the Indians. In this war several mountaineers and traders took a lively part in aiding the Indians with ammunition and supplies.

The murder of Capt. J. W. Gunnison and party by the Pahvantes, which occurred in November, 1853, was the direct result of the conduct of a party of emigrants from the States, on their way to California, who killed a Pahvante Indian and wounded two others at Corn creek, a short time previously; according to the Indian rule of revenge, the massacre of the next white men found on their grounds was the consequence.

In the settlement of new valleys, President Brigham Young and the leading authorities of the Church have invariably counseled the settlers to build forts and locate themselves in sufficient numbers and in such a manner that when Indians were disposed to commit depredations they would be able to secure their families and their stock.

April 9th, 1865, several Indians visited Manti, Sanpete county; they wanted to have a big talk, and boasted of having killed fifteen head of cattle within a few days, and got into a quarrel with some of the citizens.

Next day, several of the citizens of Manti rode out to the range to find if the boasts of the Indians about killing their cattle were true, when they were confronted by the Indians, who fired upon them, killing a young man named Peter Ludvicksen. The Indians retired up Salt Creek cañon into Sevier county, where they found Elijah B. Ward and James Anderson in charge of cattle, whom they also killed. A party started on the 12th in pursuit of the Indians and the cattle which they had taken with them. This party was overpowered by the Indians, and two of their number, William Kearnes and Jens Sorensen, were killed.

May 26th, the Indians made a descent upon a family named Given, in Thistle Valley, twelve miles from Fairview, in Sanpete County, and massacred the father, mother, and four children, having the evening previous killed Jens Larsen. On the 29th they also killed David H. Jones.

In July, Robert Gillespie and Anthony Robinson were killed and several citizens wounded.

These Indian massacres, which were generally accompanied by raids on cattle, rendered it necessary for the inhabitants of Sanpete, Sevier, Piute, Millard, Iron, Beaver, Kane, and Washington counties to guard their stock with mounted, armed men.

In January, 1866, a band of Indians made a descent upon the Pipe Spring ranch, in Kane county, killing J. M. Whitmore, the proprietor, and Robert McIntire, and robbing the ranch of cattle and sheep. The ranch of Pahreah was also robbed, and besieged for several months. Peter Shirts barricaded his house, and by strategy and unceasing vigilance, with the aid of his family, managed to evade the blow aimed at him until relieved by Captain James Andrus and a company of mounted volunteers from Grafton.

April 2nd, Robert Berry and wife, with his brother Joseph, were waylaid and massacred at Short creek, Kane county.

On the 22nd, Albert Lewis was killed and three persons wounded near Marysvale, Piute county; and on the 29th, Thomas Jones was killed and Wm. Avery wounded at Fairview, in Sanpete county. On the 10th of June, the Indians made a raid on Round Valley, driving away three hundred head of cattle and horses and killing Father James Ivie and Henry Wright. On the 24th, Charles Brown was killed and Thomas Snarr wounded in Thistle Valley; and while recovering the horses and cattle driven off from the Spanish Fork pasture, John Edmiston, of Manti, was killed, and A. Dimick, of Spanish Fork, badly wounded.

Early in 1867, the continued hostile intentions of the Indians were announced in the massacre of James P. Petersen, his wife and daughter, near Glenwood, Sevier county, who were mutilated in the most horrible manner. The vigilance of the militia of these counties, assisted by detachments from counties as far north as Salt Lake and Davis, so far held the Indians in check that during the entire year there were only three other citizens killed and three of the militia, viz.: Lewis Lund, James Meek and Andrew Johansen, and Major John W. Vance, Sergeant Heber C. Houtz and Private John Hay.

· In consequence of these Indian raids and massacres the counties of Piute and Sevier were entirely abandoned, as well as the settlements of Berrysville, Winsor, Upper and Lower Kanab, Shunesburg, Springdale and Northup, and many ranches in Kane county, also the settlements of Pangwitch and Fort Sandford, in Iron county.

FOREIGN MISSIONS.

Joseph Smith, the Prophet, enjoined upon the Twelve Apostles that they should preach the gospel to all the nations of the earth, and wherever they could not go, to send the same, that all nations might be faithfully warned of the restoration of the everlasting gospel in all its purity and fulness for the salvation of mankind, and the near advent of the Messiah, preparatory to the introduction of His reign of righteousness upon the earth.

ENGLAND.—In June, 1837, Elders Heber C. Kimball, Orson Hyde, Willard Richards, Joseph Fielding and three others went to England and opened the door of the gospel to Great Britain, commencing their labors in Preston, Lancashire, and extended them to different parts of the kingdom, where they baptized about fifteen hundred persons. Elders Kimball and Hyde returned to America in April, 1838, leaving Elders Joseph Fielding and Willard Richards in charge of the Mission.

In 1840, President Brigham Young, Heber C. Kimball, Parley P. Pratt, Orson Pratt, John Taylor, Wilford Woodruff and George A. Smith, of the Quorum of the Twelve Apostles, proceeded to England and ordained Willard Richards an apostle, he having been previously called to that office by revelation. They preached one year and fourteen days, and established branches of the Church in many of the principal cities from London to Edinburgh. They established a printing office and an emigration agency, published the Book of Mormon, Doctrine and Covenants and Hymn book, and issued sixty thousand pamphlets and the first volume of the *Millennial Star*. Seven of the Apostles returned, leaving Elder Parley P. Pratt to preside over the Mission.

Palestine.—In 1841, Elder Orson Hyde, went on a mission to Jerusalem. He remained in Bavaria until he acquired the German language and published a pamphlet which he was not allowed to circulate openly. He traveled through the Austrian and Turkish empires, visiting Jerusalem; finding the laws of all these countries so proscriptive as to prevent him from publishing or preaching the Gospel, he returned to Nauvoo in 1842.

Pacific Isles.—In October, 1843, Elders Noah Rogers, Addison Pratt, Ben. F. Grouard and Knowlton F. Hanks started on a mission to the Pacific Isles. Elder Philip B. Lewis paid their passage as a donation to the Mission. Knowlton F. Hanks died of consumption and was buried in the sea, the other three reached the Society Islands and were successful in establishing the Gospel and in baptizing upwards of twelve hundred of the natives. Elder James S. Brown, Alva Hanks, —— Whittaker and others subsequently followed to these islands, and continued their labors with commendable zeal and uniform success until the establishment of the French Protectorate; after which the French authorities expelled the Elders from the Islands, and prohibited them from ever returning, and compelled the native converts to discontinue their worship. This ocurred in the year 1851.

Notwithstanding the constant scenes of persecution and the distress incident thereto which the Saints in Illinois endured, after the return of the Twelve from England, Elders were constantly sent to preside over the conferences abroad, strengthen and encourage the native Elders and extend the work of the ministry.

Elder Wilford Woodruff went to England in 1844, and presided over the British mission. Upon hearing of the exodus of the Church from Nauvoo, he returned in 1846; when Elders Orson Hyde, Parley P. Pratt and John Taylor were sent to England. They returned early in 1847 to Council Bluffs, where they found the Saints encamped.

At the October Conference, in 1849, several of the Twelve Apostles and other Elders were sent on missions.

France—Elder John Taylor visited Paris and established a small branch of the Church, and had the Book of Mormon translated into the French language and published an edition of the same, but the stringency of the laws prohibited public meetings and measurably tied his hands. He also published a volume of a periodical entitled, *Etoile du Deseret*. The work was continued in France by Elders C. E. Bolton and L. E. Bertrand until the latter was prohibited by the Prefect of Police from preaching the Gospel or attending meetings.

Germany.—Elder Taylor also visited Hamburg, and procured the translation and publication of the Book of Mormon in the German language, and a few numbers of a periodical entitled *Zion's Panier*. In Germany, the mission was continued by Elder Daniel Carn, until expelled by the authorities of the free city of Hamburg. Subsequently, Elders George C.

Riser, J. F. Secrist and George Mayer were imprisoned and expelled the Confederation for attempting to preach.

Switzerland and Italy.—Elder Lorenzo Snow proceeded to Switzerland and Italy, and established branches of the Church and published the Book of Mormon in the Italian language, also pamphlets in the Italian and French languages. In these labors he was assisted by Elder Joseph Toronto, from Utah, and Elders T. B. H. Stenhouse and Jabez Woodard, from the British mission. Elder Stenhouse published a periodical, entitled *Le Reflecteur*, in French. Subsequently, the Swiss mission was continued by Elders Daniel Tyler and John L. Smith. Elder Tyler commenced the publication of the *Darsteller* in the German language, which was continued by Elder John L. Smith, on his first mission. On his last mission Elder Smith published *The Reform* in German. He also translated and published, in the French language, Elder Parley P. Pratt's *Marriage and Morals in Utah.* An edition of the Book of Mormon in German was also published from the stereotype plates. Some of the Cantons would not allow publishing, but allowed preaching; others prohibited preaching, but would allow publishing, and some would not allow either.

Scandinavia.—Elder Erastus Snow arrived in Copenhagen, Denmark, in June, 1850, and in September a branch of the Church was organized, which numbered fifty members. Elder Snow was accompanied by Elders P. O. Hansen and John E. Forsgren; the latter proceeded to Sweden and endeavored to introduce the work there, but was summarily banished. In 1851, Elder Snow had the Book of Mormon translated and commenced the publication of the *Skandinavien Stjerne*. He also baptized and ordained three mechanics from Iceland, and sent them to their native land to preach the Gospel. In February, 1852, the Book of Doctrine and Covenants and a large edition of the Hymn Book were published, also a pamphlet of fifty pages, entitled *A Voice from the Land of Zion*.

Chili.—In 1851, Elders Parley P. Pratt and Rufus Allen went on a mission to Chili, where they remained several months, not having the opportunity of even teaching in private, except in violation of the most rigid laws. They were obliged to return to California, where Elder Pratt continued to preach and publish until he returned to Utah.

Australia.—In 1840, Elder George A. Smith ordained William Barrett an Elder, at Burslem, England, and set him apart to a mission to South Australia. Elder Barrett proceeded thither and commenced teaching the principles of the Gospel and was enabled to sow the good seed which afterwards bore fruit.

Elders John Murdoch and C. W. Wandell arrived in Sydney, Australia, in October, 1851, and commenced to preach and publish concerning the Latter-day Work, and in January, 1852, organized a branch of the Church in Sydney, and published a pamphlet on the persecutions endured by the Latter-day Saints, and a periodical entitled, *Zion's Watchman*.

Elders Augustus Farnham, William Hyde, Burr Frost, Josiah W. Fleming and others landed at Sydney early in 1853. These missionaries extended their labors to Van Dieman's Land and New Zealand, and continued the publication of *Zion's Watchman*.

Prussia.—In January, 1853, Elders Orson Spencer and Jacob Houtz arrived in Berlin, Prussia, but found that it was impossible to preach or publish the truth of the Latter-day Work in consequence of religious intoleration. These Elders wrote to the King's Minister of Public Worship for permission to preach, but were immediately summoned before the police court and catechised as to the object of their mission. They were ordered to leave the kingdom next morning, under penalty of transportation.

Gibraltar.—Elders Edward Stevenson and N. T. Porter arrived in Gibraltar in March, 1853, and were immediately summoned to appear before the police and establish their right to remain on the Rock. Elder Porter was required to leave, but Elder Stevenson having been born there maintained his right to remain, but the Governor forbade his preaching "Mormonism." He, however, remained over a year and baptized several amidst threats, prohibitions and constant opposition. He also endeavored to open up the work in Spain, but was not permitted by the authorities.

Hindostan.—Elders Nathaniel V. Jones, Robert Skelton, Samuel A. Woolley, William Fotheringham, Richard Ballantyne, Truman Leonard, Amos Milton Musser, Robert Owen, and William F. Carter arrived in Calcutta and held a Conference there April 29th, 1853. The Hindostanee. missionaries extended their labors throughout India as the way opened; but finding the Hindostanees destitute of honesty and integrity, insomuch that when converted and baptized they would for a few pice join any other religion, and finding the Europeans so aristocratic that they were hardly approachable, they left the country, after having traveled to all the principal stations in India, where frequently they were ordered out of cantonments and had to sleep in the open air, exposed to that sickly climate, to poisonous reptiles and to wild beasts. Elder William Willes, from England, had traveled up the Ganges and visited Simla, and Elder Hugh Findlay, irom the British mission, labored in Bombay and the adjacent country.

China.—Elders Hosea Stout, Chapman Duncan and James Lewis were sent to China. They reached Hong Kong April 27, 1853, but owing to the revolution spreading through that country, they were unable to go elsewhere. The inhabitants told them that they had not time to "talka" religion. The way soon opened for them to return to San Francisco, which they did in August.

Siam.—The missionaries sent in the Fall of 1852, to Siam, finding it impossible to ship thither from San Francisco, accompanied the Hindostanee missionaries to Calcutta, where, in consequence of the war in Burmah, they learned that the overland route to Siam was interrupted, when Elders Chauncey W. West and Franklin Dewey concluded to go to Ceylon, and Elders Elam Luddington and Levi Savage to Siam; by way of Burmah.

Ceylon.—The Ceylon missionaries encountered much opposition, partly caused by the circulation of a large number of tracts from Europe containing misrepresentations and lies. At Galle the newspapers advised the people not to receive "Mormon" missionaries into their houses lest they should become partakers of their evil deeds, which counsel was implicitly obeyed. The missionaries had an introduction to a gentleman living at Columbo, seventy miles distant and proceeded thither. Elder Dewey sacrificed his watch to get a little something to eat. On their return they passed through thirty-seven towns, and witnessed the immoral practices and social degradation of the inhabitants. They visited high and low, priest and people, but they would neither open their doors for preaching, nor feed the missionaries, without being well paid.

Elder Savage remained in Burmah nearly two years, without being able to establish a branch. Elder Luddington proceeded to Bankok, Siam, where he was stoned and rejected.

South Africa.—In 1853, Elders Jesse Haven, William Walker, and Leonard I. Smith arrived at the Cape of Good Hope. The first three meetings held in Cape Town were broken up by rioters. Elders Smith and Walker went into the country, where they obtained a foothold and commenced to baptize. Elder Haven remained and preached amid much opposition and raised up a branch of the Church. Elder Walker proceeded to Fort Beaufort and baptized several. Elder Smith labored around Fort Elizabeth and organized a small conference.

Sandwich Isles.—In the Fall of 1850, a number of Elders were sent to the Sandwich Islands. After laboring till April, 1851, the President of the mission and others concluded to leave. But Elder George Q. Cannon and several Elders remained, and, after acquiring the language, baptized hundreds. Elder Cannon translated and published an edition of the Book of Mormon in the Hawaiian language.

West Indies.—Elders Aaron F. Farr, Darwin Richardson, Jesse Turpin and A. B. Lambson landed at Jamaica, in the West Indies, January 10th, 1853. They called upon the American consul, Mr. Harrison, who advised them to hire a hall and announce public preaching, as the laws extended toleration to all sects, which they accordingly did; but a mob numbering one hundred and fifty persons, gathered around the building and threatened to tear it down were these polygamists, as they termed the Elders, permitted to preach therein. Unless the Elders could give security for the price of the hall the landlord objected to their holding meeting. The Elders informed him that they were not there to enforce their principles upon the people—to quell mobs, nor to protect property, but to preach the Gospel of Jesus Christ to those who were willing to hear. The Elders got away from the Island safely, though while they remained they had to run the gauntlet, and two of them were shot at by a negro.

British Guiana.—Elders James Brown and Elijah Thomas, missionaries to British Guiana, shipped from San Diego, California, to Panama, thence to Chagres and Aspinwall. From the latter port, unable to ship for British Guiana, they embarked for Jamaica. After conferring with the West India missionaries, they concluded to embark with them for Barbadoes, being still unable to ship for the point of their destination. After paying their passages they were not allowed to proceed thither; the prejudice was so great against the Elders that the harbor agent or naval officers would not allow them to be shipped to any English island. As the only alternative they proceeded to New York with the West India missionaries, where they all landed in February, 1853, and labored in the United States, except Elder Darwin Richardson, who went to England and labored there.

Malta.—In 1853, Elder James F. Bell was sent from England to Malta, where several were baptized. Upon the breaking out of the Crimean war, the interest in the work was broken off, still a few of the soldiers in the British regiments that landed there obeyed the Gospel. There originated from this mission three branches of the Church, viz.: one in Florianna, Malta; a second called the "floating branch," in the Mediterranean, which consisted of sailors belonging to Her British Majesty's ships the Bellerophon, Trafalgar, Vengeance and Brittania; a third, the expeditionary force branch in the Crimea; the latter consisted of brethren belonging to the 30th, 41st, 93d and 95th British regiments. A few of the members of these branches lost their lives in the Crimean war.

Elder Orson Pratt was sent on a mission to Austria in April, 1864. Accompanied by Elder William W. Riter he proceeded to Vienna, where they labored for several months to acquire the German language; but in consequence of religious intolerance they were unable to open the door for the proclamation of the Gospel in that country.

Immigration.—In those nations where the Gospel has been received, Elders have been sent from Utah from time to time to preach and publish and to assist the native Elders in spreading the work. A constant stream of emigration has flowed thence to the Headquarters of the Saints. From the European missions the emigration has been from two to four thousand persons annually.

The following interesting article, under the head of "Church History," is from the pen of President Joseph Smith, and was written by him in 1842 for publication in the Chicago Democrat. We copy it from the *Times and Seasons*, Vol. III, page 706:

"At the request of Mr. John Wentworth, editor and proprietor of the Chicago *Democrat*, I have written the following sketch of the rise, progress, persecution, and faith of the Latter-day Saints, of which I have the honor, under God, of being the founder. Mr. Wentworth says, that he wishes to furnish Mr. Bastow, a friend of his, who is writing the history of New Hampshire, with this document. As Mr. Bastow has taken the proper steps to obtain correct information, all that I shall ask at his hands is, that he publish the account entire, ungarnished, and without misrepresentation.

"I was born in the town of Sharon, Windsor county, Vermont, on the 23d of December, A. D. 1805. When ten years old, my parents removed to Palmyra, New York, where we resided about four years, and from thence we removed to the town of Manchester.

"My father was a farmer and taught me the art of husbandry. When about fourteen years of age I began to reflect upon the importance of being prepared for a future state, and, upon enquiring the plan of salvation, I found that there was a great clash in religious sentiment; if I went to one society they referred me to one plan, and another to another; each one pointing to his own particular creed as the *summum bonum* of perfection. Considering that all could not be right, and that God could not be the author of so much confusion, I determined to investigate the subject more fully, believing that if God had a church it would not be split up into factions, and that if he taught one society to worship one way, and administer in one set of ordinances, he would not teach another principles which were diametrically opposed. Believing the word of God, I had confidence in the declaration of James, 'If any man lack wisdom, let him ask of God, who giveth to all men liberally and upbraideth not, and it shall be given him,' I retired to a secret place in a grove and began to call upon the Lord. While fervently engaged in supplication, my mind was taken away from the objects with which I was surrounded, and I was enwrapped in a heavenly vision, and saw two glorious personages who exactly resembled each other in features and likeness, surrounded with a brilliant light which eclipsed the sun at noon-day. They told me that all religious denominations were believing in incorrect doctrines, and that none of them was acknowledged of God as His church and kingdom. And I was expressly commanded to 'go not after them;' at the same time receiving a promise that the fulness of the gospel should at some future time be made known unto me.

"On the evening of the 21st of September, A. D. 1823, while I was praying unto God, and endeavoring to exercise faith in the precious promises of scripture, on a sudden a light like that of day, only of a far purer and more glorious appearance and brightness, burst into the room, indeed the first sight was as though the house was filled with consuming fire; the appearance produced a shock that affected the whole body; in a moment a personage stood before me surrounded with a glory yet greater than that with which I was already surrounded. This messenger proclaimed himself to be an angel of God, sent to bring the joyful tidings, that the covenant which God made with ancient Israel was at hand to be fulfilled, that the preparatory work for the second coming of the Messiah was speedily to commence; that the time was at hand for the gospel, in all its fulness, to be preached in power unto all nations, that a people might be prepared for the millennial reign.

"I was informed that I was chosen to be an instrument in the hands of God to bring about some of his purposes in this glorious dispensation.

"I was also informed concerning the aboriginal inhabitants of this country, and shown who they were, and from whence they came; a brief sketch of their origin, progress, civilization, laws, governments, of their righteousness and iniquity, and the blessings of God being finally withdrawn from them as a people was made known unto me. I was also told where there were deposited some plates on which were engraven an abridgement of the records of the ancient prophets that had existed on this continent. The angel appeared to me three times the same night and unfolded the same things. After having received many visits from the angels of God unfolding the majesty and glory of the events that should transpire in the last days, on the morning of the 22d of September, A. D. 1827, the angel of the Lord delivered the records into my hands.

"These records were engraven on plates which had the appearance of gold, each plate was six inches wide and eight inches long and not quite so thick as common tin. They were filled with engravings, in Egyptian characters and bound together in a volume, as the leaves of a book with three rings running through the whole. The volume was something near six inches in thickness, a part of which was sealed. The characters on the unsealed part were small and beautifully engraved. The whole book exhibited many marks of antiquity in its construction and much skill in the art of engraving. With the records was found a curious instrument, which the ancients called 'Urim and Thummim,' which consisted of two transparent stones set in the rim of a bow fastened to a breast-plate.

"Through the medium of the Urim and Thummim I translated the record, by the gift and power of God.

"In this important and interesting book the history of ancient America is unfolded, from its first settlement by a colony that came from the tower of Babel at the confusion of languages, to the beginning of the fifth century of the Christian era. We are informed by these records that America in ancient times had been inhabited by two distinct races of people. The first were called Jaredites, and came directly from the tower of Babel. The second race came directly from the city of Jerusalem, about six hundred years before Christ. They were principally Israelites, of the descendants of Joseph. The Jaredites were destroyed about the time that the Israelites came from Jerusalem, who succeeded them in the inheritance of the country. The principal nation of the second race fell in battle towards the close of the fourth century. The remnant are the Indians that now inhabit this country. This book also tells us that our Savior made his appearance upon this continent after his resurrection, that he planted the gospel here in all its fulness, and richness, and power, and blessing; that they had apostles, prophets, pastors, teachers and evangelists; the same order, the same priesthood, the same ordinances, gifts, powers and blessings as were enjoyed on the eastern continent; that the people were cut off in consequence of their transgressions; that the last of their prophets who existed among them was commanded to write an abridgement of their prophesies, history, etc., and to hide it up in the earth, and that it should come forth and be united with the Bible for the accomplishment of the purposes of God in the last days. For a more particular account I would refer to the Book of Mormon, which can be purchased at Nauvoo, or from any of our traveling elders.

"As soon as the news of this discovery was made known, false reports, misrepresentations and slander flew, as on the wings of the wind, in every direction; the house was frequently beset by mobs, and evil designing persons. Several times I was shot at, and very narrowly escaped, and every device was made use of to get the plates away from me, but the power and blessing of God attended me, and several began to believe my testimony.

"On the 6th of April, 1830, the 'Church of Jesus Christ of Latter-day Saints' was first organized in the town of Fayette, Seneca county, State of New York. Some few were called and ordained by the spirit of revelation and prophesy, and began to preach as the spirit gave them utterance, and though weak, yet were they strengthened by the power of God, and many were brought to repentance, were immersed in the water, and were filled with the Holy Ghost by the laying on of hands. They saw visions and prophesied, devils were cast out and the sick healed by the laying on of hands. From that time the work rolled forth with astonishing rapidity, and churches were soon formed in the States of New York, Pennsylvania, Ohio, Indiana, Illinois and Missouri; in the last named State a considerable settlement was formed in Jackson county; numbers joined the church and we were increasing rapidly; we made large purchases of land, our farms teemed with plenty, and peace and happiness were enjoyed in our domestic circle and throughout our neighborhood; but as we could not associate with our neighbors—who were many of them the basest of men, and had fled from the face of civilized society to the frontier country, to escape the hand of justice—in their midnight revels, their Sabbath breaking, horse racing and gambling, they commenced at first to ridicule, then to persecute, and, finally, an organized mob assembled and burned our houses, tarred and feathered, and whipped many of our brethren, and finally drove them from their habitations, who, houseless and homeless, contrary to law, justice and humanity, had to wander on the bleak prairies till the children left the tracks of their blood on the prairie. This took place in the month of November, and they had no other covering but the canopy of heaven, in this inclement season of the year; this proceeding was winked at by the government, and although we had warantee deeds for our land, and had violated no law, we could obtain no redress.

"There were many sick, who were thus inhumanly driven from their houses, and had to endure all this abuse and to seek homes where they could be found. The result was, that a great many of them, being deprived of the comforts of life, and the necessary attendance, died; many children were left orphans; wives, widows; and husbands widowers. Our farms were taken possession of by the mob, many thousands of cattle, sheep, horses and hogs were taken, and our household goods, store goods, and printing press and type were broken, taken or otherwise destroyed.

"Many of our brethren removed to Clay, where they continued until 1836, three years; there was no violence offered, but there were threatenings of violence. But in the Summer of 1836, these threatenings began to assume a more serious form; from threats, public meetings were called, resolutions were passed, vengeance and destruction were threatened, and affairs again assumed a fearful attitude. Jackson county was a sufficient precedent, and as the authorities in that county did not interfere, they boasted that they would not in this, which, on application to the authorities, we found to be too true, and after much violence, privation and loss of property we were again driven from our homes.

"We next settled in Caldwell and Davies counties, where we made large and extensive settlements, thinking to free ourselves from the power of oppression by settling in new counties, with very few inhabitants in them, but here we were not allowed to live in peace, but in 1838 we were again attacked by mobs; an exterminating order was issued by Governor Boggs, and under the sanction of law an organized banditti ranged through the country, robbed us of our cattle, sheep, horses, hogs, etc., many of our people were murdered in cold blood, the chastity of our women was violated, and we were forced to sign away our property at the point of the sword, and after enduring every indignity that could be heaped upon us by an inhuman, ungodly band of marauders, from twelve to fifteen thousand souls, men, women and children, were driven from their own firesides, and fr in lands that they had warantee deeds of, houseless, friendless and homeless, (in the depth of winter,) to wander as exiles on the earth or to seek an asylum in a more genial clime, and among a less barbarous people.

"Many sickened and died, in consequence of the cold and hardships they had to endure; many wives were left widows, and children orphans, and destitute. It would take more time than is allotted me here to describe the injustice, the wrongs, the murders, the bloodshed, the theft, misery and woe that have been caused by the barbarous, inhuman and lawless proceedings in the State of Missouri.

"In the situation before alluded to we arrived in the State of Illinois in 1839, where we found a hospitable people and a friendly home; a people who were willing to be governed by the principles of law and humanity. We have commenced to build a city called 'Nauvoo,' in Hancock county, we number from six to eight thousand here, besides vast numbers in the county around and in almost ever county of the State. We have a city charter granted us and a charter for a Legion, the troops of which now number 1,500. We have also a charter for a university, for an agricultural and manufacturing society, have our own laws and administrators, and possess all the privileges that other free and enlightened citizens enjoy.

"Persecution has not stopped the progress of truth, but has only added fuel to the flame: it has spread with increasing rapidity. Proud of the cause which they have espoused, and conscious of their innocence and of the truth of their system, amidst calumny and reproach have the elders of this church gone forth and planted the gospel in almost every State in the Union. It has penetrated our cities, it has spread over our villages, and has caused thousands of our intelligent, noble and patriotic citizens to obey its divine mandates, and be governed by its sacred truths. It has also spread into England, Ireland, Scotland and Wales; in the year of 1840, when a few of our missionaries were sent over five thousand joined the standard of truth; there are numbers now joining in every land.

"Our missionaries are going forth to different nations, and in Germany, Palestine, New Holland, the East Indies, and other places, the standard of truth has been erected; no unhallowed hand can stop the work from progressing. Persecutions may rage, mobs may combine, armies may assemble, calumny may defame, but the truth of God will go forth boldly, nobly and independently, till it has penetrated every continent, visited every clime, swept every country, and sounded in every ear, till the purposes of God shall be accomplished and the Great Jehovah shall say the work is done.

"We believe in God, the Eternal Father, and in His Son, Jesus Christ, and in the Holy Ghost.

"We believe that men will be punished for their own sins and not for Adam's transgression.

"We believe that through the atonement of Christ all mankind may be saved by obedience to the laws and ordinances of the Gospel.

"We believe that these ordinances are: First, Faith in the Lord Jesus Christ; second, Repentance; third, Baptism by immersion for the remission of sins; fourth, Laying on of Hands for the Gift of the Holy Ghost.

"We believe that a man must be called of God, by 'prophesy, and by laying on of hands' by those who are in authority to preach the gospel and administer in the ordinances thereof.

"We believe in the same organization that existed in the primitive church, viz.: apostles, prophets, pastors, teachers, evangelists, etc.

"We believe in the gift of tongues, prophesy, revelation, visions, healing, interpretation of tongues, etc.

"We believe the Bible to be the word of God, as far as it is translated correctly; we also believe the Book of Mormon to be the word of God.

"We believe all that God has revealed, a l that He d es now reveal, and we believe that He will yet reveal many great and important things pertaining to the Kingdom of God.

"We believe in the literal gathering of Israel and in the restoration of the Ten Tribes. That Zion will be built upon this continent. That Christ will reign personally upon the earth, and that the earth will be renewed and receive its paradisaic glory.

"We claim the privilege of worshipping Almighty God according to the dictates of our conscience, and allow all men the same privilege, let them worship how, where, or what they may.

"We believe in being subject to kings, presidents, rulers and magistrates, in obeying, honoring and sustaining the law.

"We believe in being honest, true, chaste, benevolent, virtuous, and in in doing good to *all men;* indeed we may say that we follow the admonition of Paul, 'We believe all things, we hope all things,' we have endured many things and hope to be able to endure all things. If there is anything virtuous, lovely or of good report or praiseworthy, we seek after these things.

Respectfully, etc.,

JOSEPH SMITH."

REVELATION ON CELESTIAL MARRIAGE,

GIVEN TO JOSEPH SMITH, NAUVOO, JULY 12TH, 1843.

Verily, thus saith the Lord unto you, my servant Joseph, that inasmuch as you have inquired of my hand, to know and understand wherein I, the Lord, justified my servants Abraham, Isaac and Jacob; as also Moses, David and Solomon, my servants, as touching the principle and doctrine of their having many wives, and concubines: Behold! and lo, I am the Lord thy God, and will answer thee as touching this matter: Therefore, prepare thy heart to receive and obey the instructions which I am about to give unto you; for all those who have this law revealed unto them, must obey the same; for behold! I reveal unto you a new and an everlasting covenant; and if ye abide not that covenant, then are ye damned; for no one can reject this covenant, and be permitted to enter into my glory; for all who will have a blessing at my hands, shall abide the law which was appointed for that blessing, and the conditions thereof, as was instituted from before the foundation of the world: and as pertaining to the new and everlasting covenant, it was instituted for the fulness of my glory; and he that receiveth a fulness thereof, must, and shall abide the law, or he shall be damned, saith the Lord God.

And verily I say unto you, that the conditions of this law are these:— All covenants, contracts, bonds, obligations, oaths, vows, performances, connections, associations, or expectations, that are not made, and entered into, and sealed, by the Holy Spirit of promise, of him who is anointed, both as well for time and for all eternity, and that too most holy, by revelation and commandment, through the medium of mine anointed, whom I have appointed on the earth to hold this power, (and I have appointed unto my servant Joseph to hold this power in the last days, and there is never but one on the earth at a time, on whom this power and the keys of this Priesthood are conferred,) are of no efficacy, virtue or force, in and after the resurrection from the dead; for all contracts that are not made unto this end, have an end when men are dead.

Behold! mine house is a house of order, saith the Lord God, and not a house of confusion. Will I accept of an offering, saith the Lord, that is not made in my name! Or, will I receive at your hands that which I have not appointed! And will I appoint unto you, saith the Lord, except it be by law, even as I and my Father ordained unto you, before the world was! I am the Lord thy God, and I give unto you this commandment, that no man shall come unto the Father but by me, or by my word, which is my law, saith the Lord; and everything that is in the world, whether it be ordained of men, by thrones, or principalities, or powers, or things of name, whatsoever they may be, that are not by me, or by my word, saith the Lord, shall be thrown down, and shall not remain after men are dead, neither in nor after the resurrection, saith the

Lord your God; for whatsoever things remaineth, are by me; and whatsoever things are not by me, shall be shaken and destroyed.

Therefore, if a man marry him a wife in the world, and he marry her not by me, nor by my word; and he covenant with her so long as he is in the world, and she with him, their covenant and marriage is not of force when they are dead, and when they are out of the world; therefore, they are not bound by any law when they are out of the world; therefore, when they are out of the world, they neither marry, nor are given in marriage; but are appointed angels in heaven, which angels are ministering servants, to minister for those who are worthy of a far more, and an exceeding, and an eternal weight of glory; for these angels did not abide my law, therefore they cannot be enlarged, but remain separately and singly, without exaltation, in their saved condition, to all eternity, and from henceforth are not Gods, but are angels of God, forever and ever.

And again, verily I say unto you, if a man marry a wife, and make a covenant with her for time and for all eternity, if that covenant is not by me, or by my word, which is my law, and is not sealed by the Holy Spirit of promise, through him whom I have anointed and appointed unto this power,—then it is not valid, neither of force when they are out of the world, because they are not joined by me, saith the Lord, neither by my word; when they are out of the world, it cannot be received there, because the angels and the Gods are appointed there, by whom they cannot pass; they cannot, therefore, inherit my glory, for my house is a house of order, saith the Lord God.

And again, verily I say unto you, if a man marry a wife by my word, which is my law, and by the new and everlasting covenant, and it is sealed unto them by the Holy Spirit of promise, by him who is anointed, unto whom I have appointed this power, and the keys of this Priesthood; and it shall be said unto them, ye shall come forth in the first resurrection; and if it be after the first resurrection, in the next resurrection; and shall inherit thrones, kingdoms, principalities, and powers, dominions, all heights, and depths—then shall it be written in the Lamb's Book of Life, that he shall commit no murder whereby to shed innocent blood, and if ye abide in my covenant, and commit no murder whereby to shed innocent blood, it shall be done unto them in all things whatsoever my servant hath put upon them, in time, and through all eternity, and shall be of full force when they are out of the world; and they shall pass by the angels, and the Gods, which are set there, to their exaltation and glory in all things, as hath been sealed upon their heads, which glory shall be a fulness and a continuation of the seeds forever and ever.

Then shall they be Gods, because they have no end; therefore shall they be from everlasting to everlasting, because they continue; then shall they be above all, because all things are subject unto them. Then shall they be Gods, because they have all power, and the angels are subject unto them.

Verily, verily I say unto you, except ye abide my law, ye cannot attain to this glory; for strait is the gate, and narrow the way that leadeth unto the exaltation and continuation of the lives, and few there be that find it, because ye receive me not in the world; neither do ye know me. But if ye receive me in the world, then shall ye know me, and shall receive your exaltation, that where I am, ye shall be also. This is eternal lives, to know the only wise and true God, and Jesus Christ, whom He hath sent. I am He. Receive ye, therefore, my law. Broad is the gate, and wide the way that leadeth to the death; and many there are that go in thereat; because they receive me not, neither do they abide in my law.

Verily, verily I say unto you, if a man marry a wife according to my word, and they are sealed by the Holy Spirit of promise, according to mine appointment, and he or she shall commit any sin or transgression of the new and everlasting covenant whatever, and all manner of blasphemies, and if they commit no murder, wherein they shed innocent blood—yet they shall come forth in the first resurrection, and enter into their exaltation; but they shall be destroyed in the flesh, and shall be delivered unto the buffetings of Satan unto the day of redemption, saith the Lord God.

The blasphemy against the Holy Ghost, which shall not be forgiven in the world, nor out of the world, is in that ye commit murder, wherein ye shed innocent blood, and assent unto my death, after ye have received my new and everlasting covenant, saith the Lord God ; and he that abideth not this law, can in no wise enter into my glory, but shall be damned, saith the Lord.

I am the Lord thy God, and will give unto thee the law of my Holy Priesthood, as was ordained by me, and my Father, before the world was. Abraham received all things, whatsoever he received, by revelation and commandment, by my word, saith the Lord, and hath entered into his exaltation, and sitteth upon his throne. ʻ

Abraham received promises concerning his seed, and of the fruit of his loins,—from whose loins ye are, namely, my servant Joseph,—which were to continue so long as they were in the world; and as touching Abraham and his seed, out of the world they should continue; both in the world and out of the world should they continue as innumerable as the stars; or, if ye were to count the sand upon the sea shore, ye could not number them. This promise is yours, also, because ye are of Abraham, and the promise was made unto Abraham ; and by this law are the continuation of the works of my Father, wherein He glorifieth Himself. Go ye, therefore, and do the works of Abraham ; enter ye into my law, and ye shall be saved. But if ye enter not into my law, ye cannot receive the promise of my Father, which He made unto Abraham.

God commanded Abraham, and Sarah gave Hagar to Abraham to wife. And why did she do it? Because this was the law, and from Hagar sprang many people. This, therefore, was fulfilling, among other things, the promises. Was Abraham, therefore, under condemnation ? Verily, I say unto you, *Nay;* for I, the Lord, commanded it. Abraham was commanded to offer his son Isaac ; nevertheless, it was written, thou shalt not kill. Abraham, however, did not refuse, and it was accounted unto him for righteousness.

Abraham received concubines, and they bare him children, and it was accounted unto him for righteousness, because they were given unto him, and he abode in my law, as Isaac also, and Jacob did none other things than that which they were commanded; and because they did none other things than that which they were commanded, they have entered into their exaltation, according to the promises, and sit upon thrones, and are not angels, but are Gods. David also received many wives and concubines, as also Solomon and Moses my servants ; as also many others of my servants, from the beginning of creation until this time ; and in nothing did they sin, save in those things which they received not of me.

David's wives and concubines were given unto him, of me, by the hand of Nathan, my servant, and others of the Prophets who had the keys of this power ; and in none of these things did he sin against me, save in the case of Uriah and his wife ; and, therefore, he hath fallen from his exaltation, and received his portion ; and he shall not inherit them out of the world ; for I gave them unto another, saith the Lord.

I am the Lord thy God, and I gave unto thee, my servant Joseph, an appointment, and restore all things; ask what ye will, and it shall be given unto you according to my word : and as ye have asked concerning adultery,—verily, verily I say unto you, if a man receiveth a wife in the new and everlasting covenant, and if she be with another man, and I have not appointed unto her by the holy anointing, she hath committed adultery, and shall be destroyed. If she be not in the new and everlasting covenant, and she be with another man, she has committed adultery; and if her husband be with another woman, and he was under a vow, he hath broken his vow, and hath committed adultery, and if she hath not committed adultery, but is innocent, and hath not broken her vow, and she knoweth it, and I reveal it unto you, my servant Joseph, then shall you have power, by the power of my Holy Priesthood, to take her, and give her unto him that hath not committed adultery, but hath been faithful; for he shall be made ruler over many; for I have conferred upon you the keys and power of the Priesthood, wherein I restore all things, and make known unto you all things in due time.

And verily, verily I say unto you, that whatsoever you seal on earth, shall be sealed in heaven; and whatsoever you bind on earth, in my name, and by my word, saith the Lord, it shall be eternally bound in the heavens; and whosesoever sins you remit on earth, shall be remitted eternally in the heavens; and whosesoever sins you retain on earth, shall be retained in heaven.

And again, verily I say, whomsoever you bless, I will bless, and whomsoever you curse, I will curse, saith the Lord; for I, the Lord, am thy God.

And again, verily I say unto you, my servant Joseph, that whatsoever you give on earth, and to whomsoever you give any one on earth, by my word, and according to my law, it shall be visited with blessings, and not cursings, and with my power, saith the Lord, and shall be without condemnation on earth, and in heaven; for I am the Lord thy God, and will be with thee even unto the end of the world, and through all eternity; for verily, I seal upon you your exaltation, and prepare a throne for you in the kingdom of my Father, with Abraham your father. Behold, I have seen your sacrifices, and will forgive all your sins; I have seen your sacrifices, in obedience to that which I have told you; go, therefore, and I make a way for your escape, as I accepted the offering of Abraham, of his son Isaac.

Verily I say unto you, a commandment I give unto mine handmaid, Emma Smith, your wife whom I have given unto you, that she stay herself, and partake not of that which I commanded you to offer unto her; for I did it, saith the Lord, to prove you all, as I did Abraham; and that I might require an offering at your hand, by covenant and sacrifice: and let mine handmaid, Emma Smith, receive all those that have been given unto my servant Joseph, and who are virtuous and pure before me; and those who are not pure, and have said they were pure, shall be destroyed, saith the Lord God; for I am the Lord thy God, and ye shall obey my voice; and I give unto my servant Joseph, that he shall be made ruler over many things, for he hath been faithful over a few things, and from henceforth I will strengthen him.

And I command mine handmaid, Emma Smith, to abide and cleave unto my servant Joseph, and to none else. But if she will not abide this commandment, she shall be destroyed, saith the Lord; for I am the Lord thy God, and will destroy her, if she abide not in my law; but if she will not abide this commandment, then shall my servant Joseph do all things for her, even as he hath said; and I will bless him and multiply him, and give unto him an hundred-fold in this world, of fathers and mothers, brothers and sisters, houses and lands, wives and children, and crowns of eternal lives in the eternal worlds. And again, verily I say, let mine handmaid forgive my servant Joseph his trespasses; and then shall she be forgiven her trespasses, wherein she hath trespassed against me; and I, the Lord thy God, will bless her, and multiply her, and make her heart to rejoice.

And again, I say, let not my servant Joseph put his property out of his hands, lest an enemy come and destroy him; for Satan seeketh to destroy;

for I am the Lord thy God, and he is my servant; and behold! and lo, I am with him, as I was with Abraham, thy father, even unto his exaltation and glory.

Now, as touching the law of the Priesthood, there are many things pertaining thereunto. Verily, if a man be called of my Father, as was Aaron, by mine own voice, and by the voice of him that sent me: and I have endowed him with the keys of the power of this Priesthood, if he do anything in my name, and according to my law, and by my word, he will not commit sin, and I will justify him. Let no one, therefore, set on my servant Joseph; for I will justify him; for he shall do the sacrifice which I require at his hands, for his transgressions, saith the Lord your God.

And again, as pertaining to the law of the Priesthood: If any man espouse a virgin, and desire to espouse another, and the first give her consent; and if he espouse the second, and they are virgins, and have vowed to no other man, then is he justified; he cannot commit adultery, for they are given unto him; for he cannot commit adultery with that that belongeth unto him and to no one else; and if he have ten virgins given unto him by this law, he cannot commit adultery, for they belong to him, and they are given unto him, therefore is he justified. But if one or either of the ten virgins, after she is espoused, shall be with another man; she has committed adultery, and shall be destroyed; for they are given unto him to multiply and replenish the earth, according to my commandment, and to fulfil the promise which was given by my Father before the foundation of the world; and for their exaltation in the eternal worlds, that they may bear the souls of men; for herein is the work of my Father continued, that He may be glorified.

And again, verily, verily I say unto you, if any man have a wife who holds the keys of this power, and he teaches unto her the law of my Priesthood, as pertaining to these things, then shall she believe, and administer unto him, or she shall be destroyed, saith the Lord your God; for I will destroy her; for I will magnify my name upon all those who receive and abide in my law. Therefore, it shall be lawful in me, if she receive not this law, for him to receive all things, whatsoever I, the Lord his God, will give unto him, because she did not administer unto him according to my word; and she then becomes the transgressor; and he is exempt from the law of Sarah, who administered unto Abraham according to the law, when I commanded Abraham to take Hagar to wife. And now, as pertaining to this law, verily, verily I say unto you, I will reveal more unto you, hereafter; therefore, let this suffice for the present. Behold, I am Alpha and Omega. Amen.

We make the following extracts from a work published on "India, Ancient and Modern," by David O. Allen, D. D., Missionary of the American Board, for twenty-five years in India, etc. They are published in his work in an appendix devoted to the subject of Polygamy. This subject was taken into consideration by the Calcutta Missionary Conference, composed of Missionaries from various sects of England and America, and including Episcopalians, Presbyterians, Baptists and Congregationalists, in consequence of the application of converts in India, who had been legally married to several wives and who had given credible evidence of their personal piety, to be admitted into the church. After frequent consultations and much consideration the Conference unanimously came to the following conclusion :

"If a convert, before becoming a Christian, has married more wives than one, in accordance with the practice of the Jewish and primitive Christian churches, he shall be permitted to keep them all, but such a person is not eligible to any office in the church."

The arguments which we quote below are advanced in Dr. Allen's work as a justification of this action of the Conference of Protestant Missionaries on the subject.

"To those who have doubts in respect to the intrinsic moral lawfulness of plurality of wives as t existed among the ancient Jews, and who wish further to examine this subject, the consideration of the following extracts from a work called 'Thelyphthora,' publi hed anonymously* many years ago in England, is recommended. The author of t is work says :

"'The best and fairest, and indeed the only way, to get at the truth, on this, as on every occasion where religion is concerned is to lay aside prejudice, from whatever quarter it may be derived and let the Bible speak for itself. Then we shall see that more than one wife, notwithstanding the seventh commandment, was allowed by God himself, who, however others might take it, must infallibly know His own mind, be perfectly acquainted with His own will, and thoroughly understand His own law. If He did no' intend to allow a plurality of wives, but to prevent and condemn it, either by the seventh commandment, or by some other law, how is it possible that He should make laws for its regulation, any more than He should make laws for the regulation of theft or murder? How is it conceivable that He should give the least countenance to it, or so express His approbation as even to work miracles in support of it? For the making a woman fruitful who was naturally barren must have been the effect of supernatural power. He blessed, and in a distinguished manner owned, the issue, and declared it legitimate to all intents and purposes. If this be not allowance, what is?

"'As to the first, namely, His making laws for the regulation of polygamy, let us consider what is written in Exodus, 21:10. If he (i. e., the husband) take him another wife, (n t, in so doi g, that he sins against the seventh commandment, recorded in the preceding chapter, but), her food, her raiment, (i. e., of the first wife), and her duty of marriage, he shall not diminish. Here God positively forbids a neglect, much more the divorcing or putting away of the first wife, but charges no sin in taking the second.

"'Secondly. When Jacob married Rachel she was barren, and so continued for many years; but God did not leave this as a punishment upon her for marrying a man who had another wife. It is said, Genesis, 30: 22, that God remembered Rachel; and God hearkened unto her, and opened her womb, and she conceived and bare a son, and said, God hath taken away my reproach. Surely this passage of Scripture ought to afford a complete answer to those who bring the words of the marriage bond as cited by Christ, Matthew, 19: 5—"They twain shall be one flesh"—to prove polygamy sinful, and should lead us to construe them, as by this instance and many others the Lawgiver himself appears to have done; that is to say, where woman, not betrothed to another man, unites herself in personal knowledge with the man of her choice, let that man's situation be what it may, they twain shall be one flesh. How, otherwise, do we find such a woman as Rachel united to Jacob, who had a wife then living, praying to God for a blessing on her intercourse with Jacob, and God hearkening to her, opening her womb, removing her barrenness, and thus by miracle taking away her reproach? We also find the offspring legitimate, and inheritors of the land of Canaan; a plain proof that Joseph and Benjamin were

---

* This extraordinary work, though published anonymously, was generally understood to be written by the Rev. Martin Madan, Chaplain of the Lock Hospital, in London. He was a man of some musical talent; he composed the tunes "Denmark" and "Denbigh;" the first is commonly sung to the hymn, "Before Jehovah's awful throne;" the latter to that commencing "From all that dwell below the skies." He was also the author of a translation of Juvenal & Persius, with note, 2 vols.; "A commentary on the articles of Church of England;" "Thoughts on Executive Justice:" and "Letters to Dr. Priestly." He died in 1790.

no bastards, or born out of la~ful marriage.† See a like palpable instance of God's miraculous blessing on polygamy in the case of Hannah, 1 Samuel, i and ii. These instances serve also to prove that, in God's account, the second marriage is just as valid as the first, and as obligatory; and that our making it less so, is contradictory to the Divine wisdom.

"'Thirdly. God blessed and owned the issue. How eminently this was the case with regard to Joseph, see Genesis 49: 22-26; to Samuel, see 1 Samuel 3: 15. It was expressly commanded that a bastard, or son of a woman that was with child by whoredom, should not enter into the congregation of the Lord, even to his tenth generation (Deuteronomy 23: 2). But we find Samuel, the offspring of polygamy, ministering to the Lord in the Tabernacle at Shiloh, even in his very childhood, clothed with a linen ephod, before Eli the priest. See this whole history, 1 Samuel i and ii. Who, then can doubt of Samuel's legitimacy, and consequently of God's allowance of, and blessing on, polygamy? If such second marriage was, in God's account, null and void, as a sin against the original law of marriage, or the seventh commandment, or any other law of God, no mark of legitimacy could have been found on the issue; for a null and void marriage is tantamount to no marriage at all; and if no marriage, no legitimacy of the issue can possibly be. Instead of such a blessing as Hannah obtained, we should have found her and her husband Elkanah charged with adultery, dragged forth, and stoned to death; for so was adultery to be punished. All this furnishes us with a conclusive proof, that the having more than one wife with which a man cohabited, was not adultery in the sight of God; or, in other words, that it never was reckoned by Him any sin against the seventh commandment, or the original marriage institution, or any other law whatsoever.

"'Fourthly. But there is a passage (Deuteronomy 21: 15) which is express to the point, and amounts to a demonstration of God's allowance of plurality of wives. If a man have two wives, one beloved and another hated, and they have borne him children, both the beloved and the hated; and if the first born be hers that was hated, then it shall be, when he maketh his sons to inherit that which he hath, that he may not make the son of the beloved first-born before the son of the hated, which is, indeed the first-born, by giving him a double portion of all that he hath; for he is the beginning of his strength, and the right of the first-born is his. On the footing of this law, the marriage of both women is equally lawful. God calls them both wives, and He cannot be mistaken; if He calls them so, they certainly were so. If the second wife bore the first son, that son was to inherit before a son born afterwards of the first wife. Here the issue is expressly deemed legitimate, and inheritable to the double portion of the first-born; which could not be, if the second marriage were not deemed as lawful and valid as the first.

"'Fifthly. To say that a plurality of wives is sinful, is to make God the author of sin: for, not to forbid that which is evil but even to countenance and promote it, is being so far the author of it, and accessory to it in the highest degree. And shall we dare to say, or even think, that this is chargeable upon Him, who is of purer eyes than to behold evil, and who cannot look on iniquity? (Habbakuk 1: 13.) God forbid.

"When God is upbraiding David, by the prophet Nathan, for his ingratitude to his Almighty benefactor (2 Samuel xii.) He does it in the following terms:— verse 8,—I gave thee thy master's house, and thy master's wives unto thy bosom, and I gave thee the house of Israel and Judah, and if that had been too little, I would moreover have given thee such and such things.

"Can we suppose God giving more wives than one into David's bosom, who already had more than one, if it was sin in David to take them? Can we imagine that God would thus transgress (as it were) His own commandment in one instance, and so severely reprove and chastise David for breaking it in another? Is it not rather plain, from the whole transaction, that David committed mortal sin in taking another living man's wife, but not in taking the

† If polygamy was unlawful, then Leah was the only wife of Jacob, and none but her children were legitimate. Rachel as well as Bilhah and Zilpah were mere y mistresses and their children six in number were bastards, the offspring of adulterous connection. And yet there is no intimation of any such views and feelings in Laban's family, or in Jacob's fami y, or in Jewish history. Bilhah and Zilpah are called Jacob's wives (Genesis 37: 2). God honored the sons of Rachel, Bilhah, and Zilpah equa..y with the sons of Leah, made them the patriarchs of seven of the tribes of the nation, and gave them equal inheritance in Canaan.—D. O. ALLEN.

widows of the deceased Saul? and thus, therefore, though the law of God condemned the first, yet it did not condemn the second?

"'Sixthly. When David took the wife of Uriah, he was severely reprimanded by the prophet Nathan; but after Uriah's death, he takes the same woman, though he had other wives before, and no fault is found with him; nor is he charged with the least flaw or insincerity in his repentance on that account. The chi d which was the fruit of his intercourse with Bathsheba, during her husband Uriah's life, od struck to death with his own hand (2 Samuel 12: 15.) Solomon, born of the same woman, begotten by the same man, in a state of a plurality of wives, is acknowledged by God himself as David's lawful issue (1 Kings 5: 5,) and as such set upon his throne. The law which positively excluded bastards, or those born out of lawful wedlock, from the congregation of the Lord, even to the tenth generation, (Deuteronomy 23: 2,) is wholly inconsistent with Solomon being employed to build God's temple —being the mouth of the people to God in prayer - and offering sacrifices in the Temple at its dedication—unless David's marriage with Bathsheba was a lawful marriage—Solomon, the lawful issue of that marriage—consequently a plurality of wives no sin, either against the primary institut on of marriage, or against the seventh commandment. But so far from Solomon being under any disqualification from the law above mentioned, he is appointed by God himself to build the Temple (1 Kings 8: 19.) His prayer is heard, and the house is hallowed (chapter 9: 3,) and filled with such glory, that the priests could not stand to minister (c apter 8: 11.) Solomon, th refore, as well as Samuel, stands as demonstrable proof, that a child born under the circumstances of a plurality of wives is no bastard—God himself being the judge, whose judgment is according to truth.

"'A more striking instance of God's thoughts on the total difference between a plurality of wives and adultery, does not meet us anywhere with more force and clearness in any part of the sacred history, than in the account which is given us of David and Bathsheba, and their issue.

"'When David took Bathsheba, she was another man's wife, the child which he begat by her in that situation was begotten in adultery—and the thing which David had done displeased the Lord (2 Samuel 11: 27.) And what was the consequence? We are told, 2 Samuel 12: 1, the Lord sent Nathan the prophet unto David. Nathan opened his commission with a most beautiful parable, descriptive of David's crime; this parable the prophet applies to the conviction of the delinquent, sets it home upon his conscience, brings him to repentance, and the poor penitent finds mercy—his life is spared, verse 13. Yet God will vindicate the honor of His moral government, and that in the most awful manner—the murder of Uriah is to be visited upon David and his house. The sword shall never depart from thine house, verse 10. The adultery with Bathsheba was to be retaliated in the most aggravated manner. Because thou hast despised me, and hast taken the wife of U iah the Hittite to be thy wife, thus saith the Lord, I will raise up evil against thee out of thine own house, and I will take thy wives and give them unto thy neighbor before thine eyes; and he shall lie with thy wives in the sight of the Sun; for thou didst it secretly, but I will do this thing before all Israel, and before the Sun. All this was shortly fulfilled in the rebellion and incest of Absalom, chapter 16: 21, 22. And this was done in the way of judgment on David for taking and defiling the wife of Uriah, and was included in the curses threatened (Deuteronomy 28: 30) to the despisers of God's laws.

"'As to the issue of David's adulterous commerce with Bathsheba, it is written, 2 Samuel 12: 15, The Lord struck the child that Uriah's wife bare unto David, and it was very sick. What a dreadful scourge this was unto David, who could not but read his crime in his punishment, the fol owing verses declare—wherein we find David almost frantic with grief. However the child's sickness was unto death, for, verse 18, on the seventh day the child d ed.

"'Now let us take a view of David's act of taking a plurality of wives, when, after Uriah's death, he added Bathsheba to his other w ves (verses 24, 25.) And David comforted Bathsheba his wife, and went in unto her and lay with her, and she bare a son, and he ca led his name Solomon (that maketh peace and reconciliation or recompense,) and the Lord loved him. Again we find Nathan, who had been sent on the former occa ion, sent also on this, but with a very different message. And He (the Lord) sent by the hand of Nathan the prophet, and he called his name Jedediah (Dilectus Domini—Beloved of the

Lord,) because of the Lord,—*i. e.*, because of the favor God had towards him (verse 24.)

" Let any read onward through the whole history of Solomon ; let them consider the instances of God's peculiar favor towards him already mentioned, and the many others that are to be found in the account we have of him; let them compare God's dealings with the unhappy issue of David's adultery, and this happy offspring of Bathsh ba, one of his many wives, and if the allowance and approbation of the latter doth not as clearly appear as the condemnation and punishment of the former, surely all distinction and difference must be at an end, and the Scripture itself lose the force of its own evidence.

"'Seventhly. I have mentioned the law being explained by the prophets. These were extraordina'y messengers whom God raised up and sent forth under a special commission, not only to foretell things to come, but to preach to the peopl-, to hold forth the law, to point out their defections from it, and to call them to repentance, under the severest terms of God's displeasure unless they obeyed. Their commission, in these respects, we find recorded in Isaiah 58: 1, 'Cry aloud, spare not, lift up thy voice like a trumpet: show my people ther transgression, and the house of Jacob their sins.' This commission was to be faithfully executed at the peril of the prophet's own destruction, as appears from the solemn charge given to Ezekiel, chapter 3: 18, When I say to the wicked, 'Thou shalt surely die, and thou givest him not warning, nor speak st to warn the wicked to save his life, the -ame wicked man shall die in his iniquity, but his blood will I require at thine hand.'

"'These prophets executed their commissions very unfaithfully towards God and the people, as well as most dangerously for themselves, if a plurality of wives was sin against God's law, for it was the common practice of the whole nation, from the prince on the throne to the lowest of the people; and yet neither Isaiah, Jeremiah, nor any of the prophets, bore the least testimony against it. They reproved them sharply and plainly for defiling their neighbors' wives, as Jeremiah 5 : 8; 29; 23, in which fifth chapter we not only find the prophet bearing testimony against adultery, but against whoredom and fornication (verse 7,) for that they assembled themselves by troops in the harlots' houses Not a word against polygamy. How is it possible, in any reason, to think that this, if a sin, should never be mentioned as such by God, by Moses, or any of the prophets?

"'Lastly. In the Old Te tament, plural marriage was not only allowed in all cases, but in some commanded. Here for example, is the law (Deut. 25 : 5—10). If breth en dwell together, and one of them die and have no child, the wife of the dead shall not marry without unto a stranger: her husband's brother shall go in unto her, and take her to him to wife, and perform the duty of a husband's brother unto her. And it shall be that the first-born that she beareth shall succeed in the name of the brother which is dead, that his name be not put out of Israel, etc.

"'This law must certainly be looked upon as an exception from the general law (Leviticus 18: 16,) and the reason of it appears in the law itself, namely, 'To preserve inheritances in the families to which they belonged.'

. . As there was no law against plurality of wives, there was nothing to exempt a married man from the obligation of marrying his brother's widow. . . . . For, let us suppose that not only the surviving brother, but all the near kinsmen, to whom the marriage of the widow and the redemption of the inheritance belonged, were married men—if that exempted them from the obligation of this law—as they could not redeem the inheritance unless they married the widow (Ruth 4 : 5)—the widow be tempted to marry a stranger—to put herself and the inheritance into his hands—and the whole reason assigned for the law itse f, that of raising up seed to the deceased, to preserve the inheritance in his family, that his name be not put out of Israel—fall to the ground. For which weighty reasons, as there was evidently no law against a plurality of wives, there could be no exemption of a man from the positive duty of this law because he was married. As we say, Ubi cadit ratio, ibi idem jus.'''

" I will now hasten to the examination of a no'ion, which I fear is too common among us, and on which what is usually said and thought on the subject of a plurality of wives, i- for the most part built; I mean that of representing Christ as appearing in the world, as "a new lawgiver, who was to introduce a more pure and pe fect system of morality, than that of the law which was given by

Mose ,"—Thi horrible blasphemy against the holiness and perfection of God's law, as well as against the truth of Christ, who declared that He came not to destroy the law, but to fulfil it—this utter contradiction both of the law and the Gospel—was the foundation on which the heritic Soc nus built all his other abominable errors.

"Christ most solemnly declared—that heaven and earth could sooner pass, than one jot or tittle pass from the law—Think not, said He, that I am come to destroy the law or the prophets; I am not come to destroy, but to fulfil. So far from abrogating the law, or rule of life, which had been delivered by the hand of Moses, or setting up a new law in opposition to it—He came into the world to be subject to it in all things, and so to fulfil the whole righteousness of it. Matthew 3: 15. To magnify and make it honorable. Isaiah 13: 21, even by His obedience unto death. Speaking in the spirit of prophecy (Psalms 40: 8.) He says—Lo- I come - in the volume of the book it is written of me —I delight to do thy will. O my God; yea, Thy law is within my heart. And in His public ministry, how uniformly doth He speak the same thing?

"If we attend to our Savior's preaching, and especially to that heavenly discourse delivered from the Mount, we shall find him a most zealous advocate for the law of God, as delivered by Moses. We sha l find Him stripping it of the false glosses, by which the Jewish rabbies had obscured or perverted its meaning, and restoring it to that purity and spirituality by which it reacheth even te the thoughts and intents of the heart. For instance, when He is about to enter upon a faithful exposition of the moral law, lest his hearers should imagine, that what He was about to say, was contrary to the law of the Old Testament, being so different from the teachings of the Scribes and Pharisees, He prefaces His discourse with those remarkable words—Matthew 5: 17—20. Think not that I am come to destroy the law or the prophets, I am not come to destroy, but to fulfil; for verily I say unto you, till heaven and earth pass away, one jot or one tittle shall not pass from the law, till all be fulfilled.

"Let us take a nearer and more critical view of those passages of the Gospels, in which Christ is supposed to condemn the plurality of wives as adultery. The first which I shall take notice of, as introductory to the rest is Matthew 5: 31, 32. It hath been said, Whosoever shall put away his wife, let him give her a writing of divorcement. But I say unto you, that whosoever shall put away his wife, saving for the cause of fornication, causeth her to commit adultery, and whosoever shall marry her that is divorced, committeth adultery.

"The next scripture to be farther considered, is Matthew 19: 9. I say unto you, Whosoever shall put away his wife, (except it be for fornication) and shal marry another, committeth adultery, and whoso marrieth her which is put away, committeth adultery.

"Christ was surrounded at this time by a great multitude of people, who, in principle, as living under the law of the old Testament, were polygamists, and, doubtless, numbers of them were so in practice—many there must have been among this great multitude of Jews, who had either married two wives together, or having one, took another to her, and cohabited with both. Had our Lord intended to have condemned such practices, he wou'd scarcely have made use of words which did not describe their situation, but of words that did. It is very plain that—He that putteth away his wife, by giving her a bill of divorcement—could have nothing to do with the man who took two wives together, or one to another, and cohabited alike with both   But we are apt to construe scripture, by supposing persons to whom particular things are said, were in the circumstances then, in which we are now; but it was far otherwise: they had no municipal laws against a plurality of wives, as we have. So far from it, their whole law, (as has been abundantly proved) allowed it. Which said law, and every part thereof, was, at the time Christ spake what is recorded in Matthew 19: 9, in us full force and efficacy, as at the moment after Moses had delivered it to the people. He therefore could no more state a plurality of wives as adultery by the law of Israel, than I can state it as high treason by the laws of England.

"Can it be imagined that Christ, so remarkable for his precision, so thoroughly accurate in all He said on every other point, should use so litte in this, as not to make Himself understood by His hearers? Nay—that He should observe so little precision, as not to describe an offense, which we are to suppose Him to condemn? The most flagrant instances, the most obvious and palpable definitions of a plurality of wives cannot be understood from what He says.—He that putteth away his wife, by bill of divorcement, and marrieth another—does not describe a man's taking two wives together, and cohabiting with both; nor—a man's having a wife, and taking another to her, and cohabiting with both. Such was the Old Testament plurality of wives, not the putting away one in order to take another.

"Now, if a plurality of wives were unlawful, and of course null and void before God, then was not Christ legally descended of the house and lineage of David, but from a spurious issue, n t only in the instances above-mentioned, but also in others which might be mentioned. So that when Christ is supposed to condemn a plurality of wives as adultery, contrary to the institution of marriage, and to the seventh commandment, He must at the same time be supposed to defeat his own title to the character of the Messiah, concerning whom God had sworn to David, that of the fruit of his loins, according to the flesh. He would raise up Christ to sit on His throne. See Acts 2: 30, with Psalms 132: 11.

"The lawfulness of a plurality o wives must of course be established, or the whole of Christianity must fall to the ground, and Christ not be He that was to come, but we must look for another. Matthew 11: 3.

"The learned Selden has proved, in his Uxor Hæbraica; that a plurality of wives was allowed, not only among the Hebrews, but among most other nations throughout the world; doubtless among the inhabitants of that vast tract of Asia, throughout which the Gospel was preached by the great apostle of the Gentiles where so many Christian churches were planted, as well as in the neighboring states of Greece: yet in none of St. Paul's epistles nor in the seven awful epistles which St. John was commanded to write to the seven churches in Asia, is a plurality of wives found amongst the crimes for which they were reproved. Every other species of commerce between the sexes, is distinctly and often mentioned, this not once except on the woman's side, as Romans 7: 3; but had it been sinful and against the law on the man's side, it is inconceivable that it should not have been mentioned on both sides equally.

"Grotius observes, 'Among the Pagans, few nations were content with one wife;' and we do not find the apostle making this any bar to church-membership. It can hardly be supposed, that if a plurality of wives were sinful, that is to say, an offense against the law of God, the great apost e should be so liberal and so particular, in his epistle to the Corinthians, in the condemnation of every other species of illicit commerce between the sexes, and yet omit this in the black catalogue, chapter 6: 9, etc., or that he should not be as zealous for the honor of the law of marriage, and of the seventh commandment, which was evidently to maintain it, as Ezra was for that positive law of Deuteronomy 7: 3. against the marrying with heathens. Ezra made the Jews put away the wives which they had illegally taken, and even the very children which they had by them; how is it that Paul, if a plurality of wives was sinful, did not make the Gentile and the Jewish converts put away every wife, but the first, and annul every other contract.

"No man could have a fairer opportunity to bear his testimony against a national sin, than the Baptist had; for it is said (Matthew 3: 5) Then went out to him Jerusalem and all Judea, and all the region round about Jordan; and among the numbers who were baptiz d of him in Jordan, confessing their sins (verse 6.) there were many harlots (chapter 21: 32.) So that it is evident he did not spare to inveigh most sharply against the sin of fleshly uncleanliness; had a plurality of wives been of this kind, he doubtless would have preached against it, which, if he had, some trace would most probably have been left of it, as there is of his preaching against the sin of whoredom, by the harlots being said to believe on him; which they certainly would not have done, any more than the Scribes and Pharisees (Matthew 21: 32) if the preacher had not awakened them to a deep and real sense of their guilt, by setting forth the heinousness of their sin. He exerted his eloquence also against public grievances, such as the extortion of the public officers of the revenue—the publicans—tax-gatherers- -likewise against the oppressive methods used by the soldiery, who made it a custom either to take people's goods by violence, or to defraud them of their property, by extorting it under the terror of false accusation. These were public grievances, against which the Baptist bore so open a testimony, that the publicans and soldiers came to him, saying: What shall we do? This being the case, is it conceivable that a man of the Baptist's character, who was so zealous for the honor of the law, as to reprove even a king to his face for adultery, should suffer; if a plurality of wives be adultery, a whole nation, as it were, of public adulterers, to stand before him, and not bear the last testimony against them? I do not say this is a conclusive, but it is surely a very strong presumptive argument, that in the Baptist's views of the matter, a plurality of wives, whoredom, and adultery were by no means the same thing.

"While this system of a plurality of wives was reverenced and observed, we read of no adultery, whoredom, and common prostitution of women among the daughters of Israel; no brothels, street-walking, venereal disease; no child-murder, and those other appendages of female ruin, which are too horrid to particularize. Nor were these things possible, which, since the revocation of the divine system and the establishment of human systems, are become inevitable. The supposing our blessed Savior came to destroy the divine law, or alter it with respect to marriage, is to suppose Him laying a foundation for the misery and destruction of the weaker sex."

Having given the above extracts from the writings of the Rev. Martin Madan, in his " helyphthora," we now make the following extracts from a tract published by the eminent divine, Bishop Burnet, who was elevated to the see of Salisbury, England, by William III., and who is described as a learned, judicious and excellent Bishop. He is known principally by his "History of the Reformation," and by that of "His own Times."

The tract was written on the question:

"Is a plurality of wives in any case lawful under the Gospel?"

"Neither is it [a plurality of wives] any where marked among the blemishes of the patriarchs; David's wives, and store of them he had, are termed by the prophet, God's gift to him: yea, a plurality of wives was made in some cases a duty by Moses' law;—when any died without issue, his brother, or nearest kinsman, was to marry his wife, for raising up seed to him; and all were obliged to obey this, under the hazard of infamy, if they refused it; neither is there any exceptions made for such as were in orried. From whence I may faithfully conclude, that what God made necessary in some cases to any degree, can in no case be sinful in itself; since God is holy in all His ways.

"But it is now to be examined, if it is forbidden by the Gospel. A simple and express discharge of a plurality of wives is nowhere to be found.

"It is true our Lord discharges divorces, except in the case of adultery, adding that whosoever puts away his wife upon any other account, commits adultery: so St. Luke and St. Matthew in one place have it—or commits adultery against her: so St. Mark has it—or causes her to commit adultery: so St. Matthew in another place.

"But, says an objector, if it be adultery then to take another woman after an unjust divorce, it will follow that the wife has that right over the husband's body, that he must touch no other.

"This is indeed plausible, and it is all that can be brought from the New Testament, which seems convincing; yet it will not be found of weight.

"For it is to be considered, that if our Lord had been to antiquate the plurality of wives, it being so deeply rooted in the men of that age, confirmed by such fashions and unquestioned precedents, and riveted by so long a practice, he must have done it plainly and authoritatively, and not in such an involved manner, as to be sought out of his words by the search of logic.

"Neither are these dark words made more clear by any of the apostles in their writings: words are to be carried no farther than the design upon which they were written will lead them to; so that our Lord being, in that place, to strike out divorce so explicitly, we must not, by a consequence, condemn a plurality of wives; since it seems not to have fallen within the scope of what our Lord does there disapprove.

"Therefore, to conclude this short answer, wherein many things are hinted, which might have been enlarged into a volume, I see nothing so strong against a plurality of wives, as to balance the great and visible imminent hazards that hang over so many thousands, if it be not allowed."

TERRITORIAL GOVERNMENT.

The organization by Act of Congress of the Territory of Utah in 1850 went into effect in 1851. By the Organic Act the executive power of the Territory is vested in the Governor, who is appointed by the President of the United States, and holds his office for four years and until his succesors is elected and qualified, unless sooner removed by the President. Until 1858 the Governor was ex-officio Superintendent of Indian Affairs. He approves the acts passed by the Legislative Assembly and fills all vacancies occurring in offices until the meeting of the Legislature. He is commander-in-chief of the militia. He may grant pardons for offences against the laws of the Territory, and reprieves for violation of the laws of the United States until the decision of the President is known. It is his duty to see that the laws are faithfully executed.

The Secretary of the Territory is appointed for the same time and in the same manner as the Governor. He records the laws and proceedings of the Legislative Assembly and the official proceedings of the Executive, and transmits copies annually of the laws and journals to the Speaker of the House of Representatives, and the President of the Senate for the use of Congress, also to the President of the United States. In case of a vacancy in the office of Governor the Secretary becomes Acting Governor.

The Legislative Assembly consists of a Council composed of thirteen members, and a House of Representatives of twenty-six members. The former are elected for two years, the latter for one year. The members of the Assembly must be qualified voters in the districts in which they reside. The apportionment of representation was made in the first instance by the Governor, and subsequently by the Assembly, by giving each district representation according to its population as nearly as may be. Each branch of the Assembly elects its own officers. The respective sessions of the Assembly are limited to forty days. The Legislative powers of the Assembly extend to all rightful subjects of legislation consistent with the Constitution of the United States and the provisions of the Organic Act. Copies of all laws passed by the Assembly and signed by the Governor are forwarded to the presiding officers of both Houses of Congress and if disapproved by that body become null and void.

The apportionment of the Legislative Assembly is as follows:
Washington and Kane counties, one Councilor and one Representative.
Beaver, Iron and Piute counties, one Councilor and two Representatives.
Millard and Juab counties, one Councilor and two Representatives.
Sanpete and Sevier counties, one Councilor and two Representatives.
Utah and Wasatch counties, two Councilors and four Representatives.
Cache and Rich counties, one Councilor and two Representatives.
Weber and Box Elder counties, one Councilor and three Representatives.
Davis and Morgan counties, one Councilor and two Representatives.
Salt Lake, Tooele, Summit and Green River counties, four Councilors and eight Representatives.

The Legislative Assembly have held seventeen sessions; and so carefully and judiciously has the legislation of the Territory been conducted: that Congress has only exercised the power of disapproval in one instance, and that for political effect, designed to interfere with the marriage rites of the Church of Jesus Christ of Latter-day Saints. This is a record of which the Territory may justly be proud. The principal body of the laws, including the civil and criminal codes and modes of procedure, were passed in Governor Young's administration and remain substantially.

The Judicial power of the Territory is vested in a Supreme Court, District and Probate Courts and Justices of the Peace. The Supreme Court consists of a Chief Justice and two Associate Justices appointed by the President of the United States for the term of four years. The Territory is divided into three Judical Districts, one of the Justices of the Supreme Court being assigned to each as a District Judge. The jurisdiction of the several courts both appellate and original and of Justices of the Peace are as limited by law; with the proviso that Justices of the Peace shall not have jurisdiction in any controversy involving the title or boundaries of land nor for sums exceeding one hundred dollars.

The Organic Act requires the District Judges to reside in their districts. The First Judicial District includes the counties of Utah, Wasatch, Sanpete, Juab, Millard, Sevier and Pi-Ute. The court is held at Manti. The Second Judicial District includes the counties of Washington, Kane, Iron and Beaver. Court is held at St. George. The Third embraces the counties of Tooele, Salt Lake, Summit, Davis, Morgan, Weber, Box Elder, Cache and Rich. Court is held at Salt Lake City.

A Probate Judge is elected for each county by the Legislative Assembly. He holds office four years and has civil, criminal and surrogate jurisdiction in cases arising in the county. There are also elected three Selectmen, a Sheriff, Treasurer, Recorder, Superintendent of the Schools and Coroner. A Justice of the Peace and Constable are elected in each Precinct.

There are in Utah thirty incorporated cities. The acts incorporating Salt Lake, Ogden, Provo and Payson cities are modeled after that of Chicago. The financial policy of the Territorial Legislature, the County Courts and municipalities, has been to keep free from debt. Appropriations are annually made by the Legislative Assembly to defray the expenses of the Supreme and District Courts, and the Penitentiary. All the salaries of officers are low. Appropriations are also made by the County Courts to defray the expenses of the Probate Courts incurred in criminal cases. The principal portion of County and Territorial revenue being applied to making of roads and the building of bridges.

Appeals may be taken from the Probate Court to the District Court and from the District to the Supreme Court. Each county elects, for the term of three years, three Selectmen, one going out of office and one being elected annually. The Selectmen, with the Probate Judge, form a County Court. They divide the county into precincts, school districts, locate the roads, define the boundaries of irrigation districts, levy the taxes, provide for the erection and keeping in repair of county buildings, and provide for estray pounds in each precinct.

The Militia of the Territory consists of the able-bodied men between the ages of eighteen and forty-five, organized into a military body known as the "Nauvoo Legion," commanded by a Lieutenant-General. The Legion is divided into military districts, each district having a commander whose rank is determined by the number of men in his district. A company consists of not less than sixty men, rank and file, a battalion one hundred and twenty men, a regiment six hundred, a brigade twelve hundred and a division two or more brigades.

The reports of the Adjutant-General for 1867 show 12,024 men, armed and equipped according to law. A great number of the newly-arrived immigrants being without arms, are not enrolled.

The field officers are, one Lieutenant-General, two Major-Generals, nine Brigadier-Generals, twenty-five Colonels, one hundred and twelve Majors with their necessary respective staff officers.

One-fifth of the militia is cavalry. There are a few companies of artillery. The infantry and cavalry have modern improved arms.

In consequence of the delay which has taken place in the publication of this pamphlet, the opportunity is afforded of appending a few miscellaneous items:

Elder Ezra T. Benson, one of the Twelve Apostles, died suddenly at Ogden, September 3d.

The Utah Central Railroad Company was organized under a general Act of Incorporation, passed at the last session of the Legislative Assembly. The ground was broken by Brigham Young, President of the Company, at Ogden, in May, 1869, connecting Salt Lake City with Ogden; —distance about forty miles. The track-laying commenced September 23d, and it is anticipated that the Road will be completed early in December; the probable cost will be $1,500,000. A railroad bridge has been constructed across the Weber river. The road has been graded principally by the inhabitants along the route.

The annual catalogue of the Deseret University for the academical year 1868-9, issued lately, shows 223 students in attendance. The principal efforts of the institution have been directed towards qualifying students to become teachers.

The Book of Mormon has been published in the Deseret character.

Union stores have been formed in nearly all the districts in the Territory. The capital used in conducting these has been subscribed in small shares by the masses, enabling the people to obtain their merchandise at low rates, thereby relieving the capital heretofore employed in this branch of business, which is now being diverted to other channels of usefulness by enlarging the manufacturing interests. The wholesale importation of goods is done by a co-operative institution.

The immigration of the present season by Railroad up to date, (Oct. 1,) is estimated at three thousand souls.

The crops have been excellent throughout the Territory, except in the counties of Cache, Washington, Kane and Iron, where the grasshoppers have destroyed the most of .he cereal crops; in Washington and Kane the cotton crop is materially lessened by the same cause.

During this season President Brigham Young, his Counselors and the Twelve Apostles have visited all the counties in the Territory, excepting three, and have held large public meetings of the people, which have excited unbounded enthusiasm.

www.ingramcontent.com/pod-product-compliance
Lightning Source LLC
Chambersburg PA
CBHW032118080426
42733CB00008B/987